Which of us moms, before we had kids, didn't swear that we'd get it right, only to find out somewhere along the way that motherhood isn't always everything it's cracked up to be? Equal parts encouraging and inspiring, *Hoodwinked* is the perfect dose of relief for any mom feeling guilty for not being able to do it all.

— RUTH SOUKUP, *New York Times* bestselling author of
Living Well, Spending Less: 12 Secrets of the Good Life

Hoodwinked reads like an encouraging letter from a friend. It is full of grace, biblical wisdom, and inspiration. Many books on motherhood leave me wondering if I'm doing it all wrong. Karen and Ruth are bravely transparent and meet us moms right where we are. This book gives us the hope and encouragement we need in the midst of weary days.

— COURTNEY JOSEPH, author and blogger at
WomenLivingWell.org / Home of Good Morning Girls

Karen and Ruth understand what it is to battle the voices of guilt, anxiety, and inadequacy that plague many mothers who want to give their best to their children. In this book they share life changing truths that all mothers can grab hold of, not just to survive the journey of motherhood but to thrive in confidence and joy.

— CHRYSTAL EVANS HURST, coauthor of *Kingdom Woman*

Motherhood is not a trick or trap—it's a calling. In our culture, moms are constantly sent mixed messages. This powerful book will help mothers walk in the truth of the gospel!

—KRISTEN WELCH, author of *Rhinestone Jesus*
and blogger at Wearethatfamily.com

Hoodwinked is a clever, insightful, and much-needed resource for moms of every age! Debunking the common myths about motherhood touched the deep insecurities I have wrestled with as a new mom. It is a beautiful book all moms should read.

—JENNIFER SMITH, author of *The Unveiled Wife:
Embracing Intimacy with God and Your Husband*

W9-AHB-657

If you've ever wondered if you are doing this mom thing right, pick up *Hoodwinked* for wise guidance, laughs, and assurance. You'll learn how to tell the difference between what's important—and what's not—in this loving guide from two moms who have been there.

—ARLENE PELLICANE, author of *31 Days to
Becoming a Happy Mom*

Moms of all seasons will find compassion for the demands of the journey as well as hope and inspiration for living faithfully as a mother. Heartwarming stories, soul-filled inspiration, and generous wisdom fill each page so that mothers will feel understood, validated, and uplifted. I love the ministry hearts of Ruth and Karen and know their stories will encourage every mom who reads this book.

—SALLY CLARKSON, popular conference speaker and author
of numerous books including *Desperate: Hope for the
Mom Who Needs to Breathe*

Hoodwinked is an excellent source of encouragement for moms. It dispels the myths that confuse us and the lies that bring us down. I can't even begin to tell you the many times I felt like a failure or how often I compared myself to other moms. If only this book had been around twenty years ago when I started raising children, I would have done things differently.

—DARLENE SCHACHT, author of *Messy Beautiful Love:
Hope and Redemption for Real-Life Marriages*

Hoodwinked is for every mother who has ever questioned her parenting ability. Ruth and Karen, a dynamic duo, have teamed up to equip women to silence the destructive motherhood myths with the freeing truth of God's Word!

—JEANNIE CUNNION, author of *Parenting the
Wholehearted Child*

Oh, how I wish I'd had this book when I first became a mom! Karen and Ruth have pulled back the curtain on the lies we tend to believe about motherhood. Even more importantly, though, they have revealed the truth that will set us free. Soak in these words, recalibrate your thinking, and be hoodwinked no more!

—JILL SAVAGE, CEO of Hearts at Home,
author of *No More Perfect Moms*

HOODWINKED

Ten Myths Moms Believe &
Why We All Need to Knock It Off

KAREN EHMAN & RUTH SCHWENK

 ZONDERVAN®

ZONDERVAN

Hoodwinked
Copyright © 2015 by Karen Ehman and Ruth Schwenk

This title is also available as a Zondervan ebook. Visit www.zondervan.com/ebooks.

This title is also available in a Zondervan audio edition. Visit www.zondervan.fm.

Requests for information should be addressed to:
Zondervan, 3900 *Sparks Dr. SE, Grand Rapids, Michigan 49546*

Library of Congress Cataloging-in-Publication Data

Ehman, Karen, 1964-
    Hoodwinked : ten myths moms believe (and why we all need to knock it off) / by
Karen Ehman and Ruth Schwenk. — 1 [edition].
        pages cm
    ISBN 978-0-310-34343-1 (softcover)
    1. Motherhood — Religious aspects — Christianity. I. Title.
    BV4529.18.E365 2015
    248.8'431 — dc23   2015015792

Published in association with the literary agency of Fedd & Company, Inc., Post Office Box 341973, Austin, TX 78734.

Cover design: Dual Identity
Cover illustrations: © bortonia/© Zuki/iStockphoto®
Interior design: Denise Froehlich
Interior illustration: © Kogytuk/www.istock.com /© ba888/www.istock.com

First printing August 2015 / Printed in the United States of America

Sep-25-2015

71395_HNC_1509

From Karen:

To Vicki, Valerie, and Veronica:
Once cousins happily playing with
our dolls; now moms prayerfully
raising our ten kids. I love you all.

From Ruth:

To Mom and in memory of
Grandma Holden: I would not be
who I am without you.

From Karen and Ruth:

To all the mamas reading this, beside us in
the trenches, trying so very hard to raise
their children for God's glory. We pray that
this book whispers hope to your heart and
realigns your thinking, as you join us in the
quest at #nomorehoodwinkedmoms.

Contents

Foreword

As my husband Val and I have raised our growing children, motherhood has changed, each phase bringing its own distinct mix of joys and challenges. And, with every stage, I have been tempted to believe some statements about mothering that just aren't true.

When our kids were born, Val and I decided that I would be home with them full-time. My days were spent with my babies and children—feeding them, teaching them (whether it was their ABCs, how to tie their shoes, or how not to fight with their siblings), and caring for their most basic needs.

Because I was not actively pursuing my acting career during this season, I was tempted to believe that I was "just a mom." Fans unknowingly solidified my feelings when they would request an autograph and then ask what new TV show I was working on. When I'd answer that I was staying home to raise my children, many times their expressions were either sour or disappointed. "Oh, so you're just a mom now?" they'd ask, as if the celebrity they just met suddenly became boring and worthless. My heart would sink, making me feel as if caring for my children didn't amount to anything. But that was a lie! Our society has perpetuated the myth that a mom at home is a second-string player. But the truth is a mother who spends her days with her children, nurturing and caring for them, is fulfilling a very important role in society. She is focusing on shaping her children for the future. What a crucial calling!

Later on, as my kids grew older and Val retired from his career as a professional hockey player, we prayerfully decided I would return to my career. With my kids all in middle or high school, and my husband at home full time, it gave me the flexibility to travel for work—whether going away for a short stint to film a movie or to cohost a talk show—as well as work "9 to 5" in our hometown at Warner Bros. Studios. A new season allowed for changes and growth within our family.

One of the many myths we moms believe is that we can have it all, all at once. But I have learned from experience that we really can't! As I wrote in my book *Balancing It All*, we can pursue our dreams and further our careers—if we'd like—but we have to learn to strike a balance which is, in essence, a juggling act. Sometimes we need to allow some spinning plates to drop. We must adjust our schedules to fit the needs of our families within each season of life. Sometimes we will need to pull back. Other times we can press forward. We can "have it all"—just not all at the same time!

When we buy into the myths of motherhood, we find ourselves distracted from our mission as moms. And we are tempted to compare ourselves to other mothers who seem to be "doing it right." If only we could learn to stop believing these lies and start living the truth! Then, not only would we be able to embrace our unique journey of motherhood, but we'd be free to really enjoy our children as well. And we might learn to support other mothers who parent a bit differently than us rather than compete with them or write them off as a friend forever.

My prayer for you, as you read this book, is that you will stop believing the lies and start living the truth—the truth about motherhood that is found in God's Word. So don't be hoodwinked, mom! You are unique and so is your motherhood journey. May you be encouraged and empowered to be the mom God created—a woman who loves and serves him faithfully as she nurtures and guides her children.

> —CANDACE CAMERON BURE, wife, mom of three, actress, producer, *New York Times* bestselling author, *Dancing with the Stars* season 18 finalist

CHAPTER 1

Hoodwinked: The Mythical Mosaic of Motherhood

Mother [Muh *ther*] —noun. A woman who does the work of twenty for free. See also saint.

As a mother, it is my job to take care of the possible and trust God with the impossible.

—RUTH BELL GRAHAM

Creeeeeak. Thunk. Creeeeeak. Thunk.

So went the old wooden teeter-totter in the neighborhood park at the dead end of our small-town street. The light green paint was peeling and the metal mechanisms were in dire need of a good oiling, but the children didn't care. They happily passed the time. Up. Down. Up. Down.

Creeeeeak. Thunk. Creeeeeak. Thunk.

A few friends and I (Karen) had gathered for an afternoon play date. It was a blustery fall day, the vibrantly colored leaves hanging on for dear life before being blown away into the crisp autumn air. As the children played on the swing set and merry-go-rounds and such, we moms chatted.

My first child had been born late in the spring. Now she sat bundled up tightly in the stroller, catching an afternoon catnap. The other mothers also had infants, but older children as well. And a few of the ladies were now approaching being the mom of a half-dozen kids.

Our conversations were all over the map. Sleep schedules. The best brand of diapers. What to do for an ear infection. (Call the doctor? Or squirt garlic oil in their ear?) And some with older children discussed what to do when your youngster has a squabble with another child at church or school. And of course we talked marriage—how to find time to make that a priority when it seemed like every ounce of physical and emotional energy was being drained from us constantly throughout the day just being a mom.

I sat there soaking it all in. As a new mom, I wanted so desperately to get this mothering thing right. And I not only wanted to get it right, I was pretty sure I already knew how to do it right. After all, I'm pretty observant. And can be quite opinionated. When I combined my observations with what I thought was the right opinion, I was pretty sure that if I just *did* all the right things on the front end, my kids would turn out wonderfully. And I was somewhat judgmental of those moms I encountered whose kids did not seem to be "turning out right."

It didn't matter that I was only about four months into my mothering gig, I was pretty confident. Well, at least outwardly. To be totally honest, at times my mind secretly migrated to a place of fear. *Am I doing this mothering thing right? Will my kids turn out okay? And am I making the right choices about how I am mothering them? And what I am feeding them? And how I am disciplining them?* But rarely did I let my guard down, exposing my insecurities or admitting my doubts. Nope. On the outside, I was calm, cool, collected, and confident. But inside my mind I had to give myself an occasional little pep talk to remind myself that I knew what I was doing.

I had a lot of other beliefs about mothering in general. Some beliefs I gathered by observation. Some were wishful thinking. Some beliefs other moms told me were true. Some I read on the pages of a popular parenting book. These beliefs Velcroed themselves to my impressionable mama mind and affected not only my perspective on mothering but also my behavior. But most of all … guess what I discovered about these beliefs?

All of them were dead wrong.

The Myths of Motherhood

These beliefs are the myths of motherhood that mess with us. That trip us up. That keep us feeling deflated and defeated. That prevent us from forging deep and meaningful relationships with other moms because we feel we have not measured up. That taunt us with wrong thinking about ourselves and about other moms. Or that put a pinch in our hearts toward our children and their behavior.

These are the myths of motherhood we will explore and dismantle together:

- ❀ Mothering Is Natural, Easy, and Instinctive
- ❀ The Way I Mother Is the Right (and Only) Way
- ❀ I Am "Just" a Mom
- ❀ Motherhood Is All-Consuming and All-Fulfilling
- ❀ A Good Mother Can Do It All, All at Once
- ❀ Motherhood Is a Rat Race
- ❀ Motherhood Is the Luck of the Draw
- ❀ Everything Depends on Me
- ❀ I Have to Do It All Right, or My Child Will Turn Out Wrong
- ❀ My Child's Bad Choice Means I'm a Bad Mom

I don't doubt that you could come up with some myths of your own, even beyond this list, because motherhood is not a playground. Oh sure, there are aspects of motherhood that are a downright delight, pieces of the motherhood puzzle that snap easily into place and make us smile. It is a deep, deep joy to be a mom. Our children often make us proud. But not all things motherly are packed with pleasure, causing us to sport a smile. A bigger-than-bite-sized chunk of our motherhood role is downright wearisome. Even worrisome. And our heart's layers can start peeling away, exposing our woe as we ride the teeter-totter of parenting. Up and down. Up and down.

Creeeeeak. Thunk. Creeeeeak. Thunk.

That is often the sound of a mom's heart as it bumps and bangs through life. And only Jesus can smooth out the ride as he allows us to gain his perspective, replacing the myths with the truth of his Word.

You Are Not Alone

Moms all over the world share this common thread of weary wondering. One minute we have it all figured out, and the next minute it all unravels. We asked over three hundred moms if they had preconceived notions of what motherhood would be like, and an astounding 83 percent answered, "Yes, absolutely!" Every single one of those moms commented that those preconceived notions were *dead wrong.* Whether it was through their judgment of other moms before they became a mom themselves, or just an ideal world of motherhood they created in their mind, there was a common thread among our sisters in the survey; a resounding chorus of feelings of loneliness, weariness, and disillusionment was expressed by these women. At the core was this, though: motherhood just isn't what they had expected, and they feel totally caught off guard and unprepared for this reality.

Sarah C. shared simply what many moms feel. "I'm not the mom I imagined I'd be. It's so hard to carry out all the ideas I had in my head. Motherhood is so much harder than I ever dreamed."

Sarah is certainly not alone. We read this same sentiment over and over again.

Cindy B. said,

> Naturally, I was going to be just like my mom.... In the sixties, my father traveled six days a week leaving my mom to raise me,

four years old, and my twin brothers, one year old. After having three children, she was skinny, gorgeous, and perfect. She was always put together with hair and makeup and a cute outfit that fell perfectly on her perfect body. Every photo of her looked like a Barbie doll, including our home, which was perfect and immaculate 24/7. To this day, I'm honestly not sure how she did it. It wasn't a phase. She is still that way in her seventies. Fast-forward twenty-five years ... I couldn't understand with just one baby at the time, what I was doing wrong. Why was I so exhausted all the time? Why would I cry at the drop of a hat? I was born to be a mom, right? Ask me as a child what I wanted to be when I grew up and I'd tell you "a mommy" without hesitation. Apparently, I was doing this mommy thing wrong. On a good day, my hair was brushed, and on a really good day, possibly my teeth! A five-minute shower was a luxury (unfortunately for my husband, it wasn't a daily luxury), but actually blow-drying my hair was not. I was supposed to fit back into my skinny jeans, like my mom, but shockingly I was still wearing my maternity sweat pants and looking six months pregnant! Sleep eluded me as did an explanation as to why I had achieved my dream of motherhood and was so clearly doing a terrible job. I questioned every choice I made because I certainly didn't know myself at all! This poor, innocent little baby girl was given a raw deal by getting me for a mother. What would become of her and how was I going to get my act together and become a REAL mother, you know, like Laura Petrie, Carol Brady, and Ma on *Little House on the Prairie*?

So how do we approach motherhood with a "right" view? How do we throw off the myths that have us all horribly hoodwinked?

Making a Mom Mosaic

It was a crisp and clear fall afternoon with ocean-blue skies and white puffy clouds that looked like spun cotton dancing in the air. My (Karen's) three young children, all elementary age, didn't put up the normal fuss getting their clothes on and their shoes tied that morning. The reason for their cooperation? It was homeschool field trip day.

Several families were going on an outing to an art exhibit an hour away from home. Field trips meant fun—hanging out with friends and learning something new. And my kids loved packing a lunch to eat with the other students when the educational part of the day was all done.

As I strolled through the art gallery that morning I saw many amazing creations. There were vibrant oil paintings on canvas. Pottery pieces crafted from common red clay. Hand-blown, shiny glass objects. Collages crafted from items found in nature, such as wood and stone and shells. But the one that most caught my eye was a breathtaking mosaic that took up an enormous spot on the museum wall.

A mosaic piece of art is a very clever creation. Hundreds of seemingly broken pieces of colored glass, stone, or other materials are purposefully put together on a flat surface, creating a collage of color. While each individual piece isn't anything spectacular on its own, when they are strategically arranged, they combine to make a simply stunning image.

If you step back and view a mosaic piece in its entirety, a picture emerges. Perhaps it is a scene from nature such as a landscape of snow-capped mountains or a deep blue ocean with colorful fish swimming about. Maybe it is a snapshot of a skyline of towering or historic buildings. But more often than not, a mosaic is crafted to depict a person or persons.

Many of us have formed a mosaic in our minds of the perfect mom. Throughout our years growing up and into adulthood, we have collected tiny pieces of colored glass that we have mentally arranged in our mind to form a snapshot of just what we think a good mother should be. When we step back and gaze at the image we have fashioned, it too can take our breath away. And by that I mean leave us huffing and puffing for air as we race to try to replicate the image in our own lives.

Was there a mom in your childhood neighborhood who always fed the kids on your block fresh-baked cookies and glasses of lemonade?

Clink.

You deposited in your mind's bank that a good mom does that effortlessly and cheerfully.

Did one of your friends in high school have a mom who not only made it to all of her children's sporting events to cheer wildly in the stands, but she also held down an important job in the corporate world?

Clunk.

Another characteristic deposited. Of course you got the strong impression that a good mom should both bring home the bacon *and* fry it up in a pan.

You picked up another piece of colored glass for the mosaic of your mind when you, as a new mom, were having trouble keeping your toddler quiet in church, but a few rows ahead of you sat a mom of a half-dozen children who never moved a muscle throughout the entire service. This made you think that a good mom must know how to keep her children quiet when the preacher is preaching.

Did you visit the home of a new friend who has children about the same age as yours? Her home was not only tastefully decorated but also void of dust and clutter-free. Your mind migrated back to the scene you left at your house that morning: breakfast dishes still on the table, peanut butter smeared on the counter, and a trail of crumbs on the floor that would make Hansel and Gretel squeal with glee. Piles of dirty laundry. Dust bunnies. Toothpaste in the sink. And toys strewn about far from their proper home in the big plastic toybox.

Piece by piece we have crafted in our imagination a stunning mosaic of just what a mom should be. But there is one teensy-weensy fact we forget about mosaic depictions of people.

They are not real.

And though a real mosaic may be lovely to look at during a leisurely stroll through a cultured art gallery, a fictitious mosaic of motherhood is a horrifying sight for a mom who is trying her best to do this mothering thing.

But it isn't just our "real life" encounters with other seemingly capable and competent women that tempt us to craft an unrealistic image in our minds. A brief walk through recent history illustrates the mixed messages mothers have been fed. Images of the perfect stay-at-home mom, the liberated and freethinking woman, and the career mom. There have been a lot of moms to choose from—and to be thoroughly confused by!

Perhaps you remember *Leave It to Beaver*? The late 1950s and early '60s gave rise to a sitcom featuring "The Beaver," a likeable elementary-aged boy who was always finding his way in and out of trouble or adventure. His mom? June Cleaver was the ultimate picture of a woman in the '50s and early '60s. She was the ideal homemaker—always proper, ever wise, and consistently reliable. She was the picture of what a mom should be. In many ways, she was a motherhood mosaic come to life on the television screen!

The late 1960s and '70s saw tremendous change in society. Previously held views on sexuality, behavior, and gender roles were undergoing a "revolution." June Cleaver seemed like a woman and mom from the dusty and distant pages of history. For so many years, women had been wrongfully denied certain rights and opportunities. Seeking equality and fair treatment, the woman of this era was freethinking, liberated, and progressive. The sitcom *Partridge Family* showcases this shift. A widowed mother, Shirley, not only raised her five kiddos alone but also worked as the leader of a musical group comprised of the clan. They traveled around in a bohemian bus performing for crowds of screaming teens. Along with managing her career, she had to deal with the ups and downs of raising a brood of kids with their own challenges and antics. Shirley seemed to do it with ease.

And then came the 1980s and '90s. The popular *Cosby Show* portrayed both the husband and the wife as financial providers. No longer was just the husband working outside the home; in many cases, the mom was as well. The message during this period was of a competent and capable career woman (hello, unflappable Clair Huxtable!), who still easily managed the majority of parental responsibilities. What was implied was that you can and should have it all!

Then there were the anti-heroines, the "realistic" moms created out of a backlash against all these perfect women. Just look at *Roseanne* and Debra Barone in *Everybody Loves Raymond*. Instead of plying their families with delicious home-cooked dinners, they burn their casseroles and unleash torrents of sarcasm and anger on their un-witting husbands.

Then in the 2000s, with the Internet and the advent of social media such as Facebook, the amazingly organized mom, the creative mom, the oh-so-spiritual mom, and the every-other-kind-of mom imag-inable migrated online and developed ten thousand faces. Not only your best friend, but also the friend back from high school and the woman you met at Bible study and the blogger you follow online are now all pushing their seemingly perfect images of motherhood at you ten times a day (or as often as you check Facebook, peruse the pins on Pinterest, or spy a snapshot on Instagram).

Where do all these images of motherhood leave us? How could women today not be a little confused on what we should do or be? The debate on womanhood and motherhood is still being waged. Just those brief and general strokes of history help us to see why understanding who we are as moms has been so difficult. The messages in our culture have not only been conflicting, they have been confusing. So if you are feeling a bit perplexed, there is good reason to be! We have formed a conflicting image in our mind from the people we've known — or the ones we spied on television or the Internet — of just how a good mom behaves.

Scriptural Standards for What Makes a Good Mom

Now let's not be so quick to just blame society at large or the Inter-net or television in particular for causing us to concoct an image of perfection in our minds. Sometimes our wrong line of thinking can be traced directly back to the lofty standard of one of the most famous females in Scripture: the woman we encounter in Proverbs 31.

Of course all Scripture is God breathed. It is useful for teaching us and training us and helping us correct our behavior (2 Timothy 3:16). It enables us to pursue godliness and to stay away from evil. Scripture is perfect. But imperfect people can put a certain—and incorrect—spin on the Scriptures. Sometimes we do it to make a point we are so desperately trying to exert. Other times we are just repeating what we have been taught in the past about a particular portion of the Bible. And sometimes the voices of past preachers and teachers echo in the chambers of our mind, and we just cannot see a passage any other way than the way we have been taught.

And the mother of all passages? (Pun *totally* intended.) It is the woman we meet in Proverbs 31.

She is iconic, making an entrance almost every Mother's Day at church or occasionally on a popular Christian-mommy blog of today. She is placed on a pedestal. Praised for all she did. We glance over those twenty-two verses in the Old Testament and wonder if the woman ever slept. (And we don't see her sipping coffee, but no way could she get through that to-do list without a little java in a jar!)

Let's pause and read about her here in the verses listed below. See if it doesn't make you just a tad bit tired noting all she seems to accomplish from dawn until dusk.

> 10   An excellent wife who can find?
>   She is far more precious than jewels.
>
> 11   The heart of her husband trusts in her,
>   and he will have no lack of gain.
>
> 12   She does him good, and not harm,
>   all the days of her life.
>
> 13   She seeks wool and flax,
>   and works with willing hands.
>
> 14   She is like the ships of the merchant;
>   she brings her food from afar.

15   *She rises while it is yet night*
        and provides food for her household
        and portions for her maidens.

16   *She considers a field and buys it;*
        with the fruit of her hands she plants a vineyard.

17   *She dresses herself with strength*
        and makes her arms strong.

18   *She perceives that her merchandise is profitable.*
        Her lamp does not go out at night.

19   *She puts her hands to the distaff,*
        and her hands hold the spindle.

20   *She opens her hand to the poor*
        and reaches out her hands to the needy.

21   *She is not afraid of snow for her household,*
        for all her household are clothed in scarlet.

22   *She makes bed coverings for herself;*
        her clothing is fine linen and purple.

23   *Her husband is known in the gates*
        when he sits among the elders of the land.

24   *She makes linen garments and sells them;*
        she delivers sashes to the merchant.

25   *Strength and dignity are her clothing,*
        and she laughs at the time to come.

26   *She opens her mouth with wisdom,*
        and the teaching of kindness is on her tongue.

27   *She looks well to the ways of her household*
        and does not eat the bread of idleness.

28   *Her children rise up and call her blessed;*
        her husband also, and he praises her:

29   *"Many women have done excellently,*
        but you surpass them all."

30   *Charm is deceitful, and beauty is vain,*
        but a woman who fears the Lord is to be praised.

31   *Give her of the fruit of her hands,*
        and let her works praise her in the gates. (ESV)

Okay. Let's break this down. This gal was seemingly incredible.

As a wife, she had her husband's trust, doing him "good, and not harm, all the days of his life." Did you catch that? *All* the days of his life (verses 11 – 12).

She certainly was a Becky home-ecky, what with all of this talk of wool and flax and spinning and making homemade ruby-red garments for her family to wear in the wintertime. She even whipped up a bedspread and yet still had time to make herself some pretty purple clothing (verses 13, 19, 21, 22).

She got up early yet stayed up late (verses 15 and 18).

She was a savvy shopper. She bought food (verse 14) and a field (verse 16). And she didn't just zip down to the corner grocery store for her food. She made an effort to go all the way across town to bring her food "from afar." And that field? It seems as if she used it to turn a profit, perhaps by selling the fruit from the vineyard she planted on it.

She even had time for charity work (verse 20). Yet she still had time to stop by the local gym on her way home to work on sculpting her arms (verse 17).

Okay. Maybe that's a stretch.

While we aren't told her particular method of mothering or what Christian self-help books she read to get her colicky baby to sleep through the night, or her strong-willed child to obey the first time, or her teen to do his chores without being asked, we are certain that she struck the parenting jackpot of wisdom. How else would your children rise up and call you blessed (verse 28)? She must have not made a single mistake in the rearing of her brood.

Of course, the Mister also had great things to say about his spouse. He praised her. Shoot. The leaders of the town even seemed to rave about her (verses 23, 31).

She wasn't lazy (verse 27). She wasn't a mom who screamed at her kids but talked to them patiently and lovingly (verse 26).

If there ever were such a thing as Wonder Woman, this gal surely was it.

Or was she?

Wonder Woman or Hoodwinked Heroine?

When reading Scripture, it is important to keep in mind not only the content but also the context. We also have to be careful not to read certain descriptions of what a person did through our modern eyes and with only our current culture in mind. We have to climb into a time capsule and venture back into history to unearth the true picture of why someone did what we read about them doing.

When we catch a glimpse of all that the woman in Proverbs 31 did to serve and provide for her family, it can seem exhausting. She made things by hand. She was responsible for food and clothing and yet still had time to have a ministry outside of her four walls. But just because this particular woman crafted clothing and bedspreads for her family, does it mean that we have to?

Perhaps in the time in which she lived and the income bracket into which she and her husband fell, she had no other choice than to sew her own clothing and make her own comforter. Do we need to look at what she did and then mimic her? Or what if she were from a wealthy family, as has been noted by biblical scholars, since in verse 15 we discover she had domestic help? Maybe she had free time on her hands and sewing was her hobby. Maybe that's it! She perused the Pinterest boards of her day each afternoon and then stitched and sewed to pass the time.

Should we select these verses that mention this mom sewing and deduce that we too must sew clothing for our family and coverings for our bed? Or is the bigger takeaway the fact that she spent her time making sure that her house was properly outfitted and her kids had adequate clothing to wear?

It is also helpful for us to know that the verses in this chapter that speak of this wife and mother were written in the form of an acrostic poem. My high school pastor first pointed this out to me when I was a teenager, and I found it fascinating.

The word *acrostic* can be defined as a poem, word puzzle, or other composition in which certain letters in each line form a word or words. In the case of the description found in Proverbs 31:10–31, each line starts with a different letter of the Hebrew alphabet. Some scholars think this was done in order to easily commit to memory the words of this poem of praise. That way it could be easily recited aloud. In fact, the Jewish tradition is that men recite this acrostic as a way to praise the women in their life — often a husband to his wife — and usually on Friday nights before the Shabbat dinner.

There might be another interesting way for us to evaluate this passage other than as a check-off list of all of the actions that any of us who want to be a good wife and mother must accomplish in each twenty-four-hour period. Perhaps in reality this was an offering of praise about one particular woman from one particular man. Most Jewish and Christian scholars agree that the person who wrote Proverbs 31 was none other than King Solomon. At the beginning of the chapter, he is identified as King Lemuel. King Solomon was also known by that name. They were the same person. And just who was the amazing mother he was writing about?

Solomon's mother was Bathsheba. Yes. The same Bathsheba, if you are not familiar with the story, who was spied bathing one day by King David as he was up on his roof. The king decided he simply must have this woman — this (ahem!) *married* woman — as his wife! She then got herself in a tangled-up mess of adultery and murder and all sorts of scandal. Yet this could be the very woman the writer of Proverbs 31 is praising.

How in the world can that be?

Think about writing a card for someone's birthday. Maybe we wouldn't be so clever as to be able to offer an acrostic poem. Maybe we simply would jot our thoughts down on a piece of paper, or tell them on their Facebook wall all the things we love about them.

Would we include the ugly parts of their life? Their mistakes? The times they screwed up? Of course not. We would pick out the very best characteristics about this person. The things that stood out to us that they did over the course of the time we have known them. Actions that were memorable. And honorable. And noble.

At the end of our poem of praise for this person, if we read it in its entirety, it might appear that our birthday friend did all of these wonderful things all in the same day. But of course she didn't. It was a snapshot of her life. The highlights. The parts you would like to mention on a Facebook post or include in your handwritten birthday card.

Only the good stuff.

That is much the way we should view Proverbs chapter 31. We don't get to see between the lines.

If we read that she does her husband good and not harm all the days of her life, it might seem like a standard to which we can never live up. But we have to also think of what each verse *doesn't* say. That verse doesn't say that she does her husband good and not harm all the days of his life *every single moment of every single day.* Of course she must have had times when she blew it. When she lost her temper or was short on patience. If she never did, well … then she would be perfect. And we know the only perfect person who ever walked the face of the earth was Jesus himself.

Let's stop using the image of perfection that has been perpetuated for decades, perhaps even centuries, about this wife and mother. Was she a fabulous mom? It seems so. But what she wasn't — was perfect. She still had bad moments. She still had flaws. She still had areas of weakness in her personality and perhaps even physically. (We think she even struggled with cellulite on her thighs, since only her strong arms are mentioned!)

Perfection or Perfected?

We moms are never going to get everything perfect. Not our homes. Not our method of discipline. Not our food. Not our schedule.

When we keep these mythical mosaics of perfection as our goal, we only set ourselves up for sure failure. We need to stop pursuing the appearance of perfection. (Yes, the *appearance* of perfection. There is no such thing as actual perfection.) We must start instead to pursue the person Jesus Christ.

Only Jesus can help us to shake off the lies and embrace the truth. Only a relationship with him can help us to truly be a better mom. He doesn't do this by allowing us to be perfect, but rather by enabling us to be perfected.

Being perfected means that we pursue being more like Christ. We let the Word of God dwell richly within our heart and then we seek to obey what it says. We learn from the examples of women in Scripture, both the good and the bad, and allow the hard lessons they learned to serve as a warning for us today. We let go of the race to replicate someone else's mothering experience and instead fasten our seatbelts and prepare ourselves for the unique ride that Jesus will take us on in this whole mothering experience.

Through each joy. Each trial. Every proud mothering moment and every discouraging disappointment. We seek to learn the lesson Christ has for us at each juncture. We get our eyes off of other mothers—whether from our past or present, in real life or on some sort of screen—and we fix our eyes upon Jesus, the author and perfecter of our faith (Hebrews 12:2).

But most importantly, we stop believing the lies. Oh, there are many! And all of these lies only serve to get us off track in our pursuit of godliness and graciousness. We need to stop latching onto the lies and start living in the truth. But sometimes the problem is that we are believing—and in essence living—a lie or two, and we don't even know it. So our first step in breaking this awful cycle—of pursuing perfection based on a bunch of myths, and then failing miserably, only to beat ourselves up, cry a little (or a lot), and then get up and try to chase perfection again—is to know the lies we are consciously or unconsciously believing.

Yes. Expose them. Destroy them. Replace them with the truth.

Are you ready to start making sense of the myths you have believed? As with all lies, there is always an element of truth. So we must be discerning. The Devil is tricky. These myths we believe are subtle twistings of the truth. Theologian Charles Spurgeon said it best: "Discernment is not knowing the difference between right and wrong. It is knowing the difference between right and almost right." Some of these myths seem almost right, but they are still dead-center wrong. And they can mess with our mothering in the most awful of ways.

So are you ready to begin uncovering the truth buried deep in some of those messages that are really myths?

Today can be your first day, your first step toward walking in greater clarity. The journey begins now. It's not too late, no matter where you are, to begin walking in the light of God's Word. Motherhood doesn't have to leave us stumbling in the dark. We have a Leader who will show us the way.

No more myths. No more mixed messages. No more conflicting images and ideals of what a woman and mom should look like.

Are you tired of being hoodwinked? Today is the day we can all begin to "knock it off!" Join us as we discover the ten myths that have left us hoodwinked, so we can stop believing the lies and start living the truth.

CHAPTER 2

Myth #1: Mothering Is Natural, Easy, and Instinctive

Mother is a verb, not a noun.

—UNKNOWN

"I can't do this anymore. I just can't do this anymore," I (Ruth) lamented to my friend.

I sat in my idling car, the phone pressed close to my ear. It was the only place I could find some privacy—and some solace. I had just had my fifth miscarriage, the last of nine pregnancies. My heart was broken and my body was weary.

Four beautiful children vied for my attention at home. Inside, I was struggling—with their incessant demands, the grief of my miscarriages, and the relentless responsibility that comes with motherhood.

The season I was in was not what I had envisioned: all those picture-perfect moments of moms snuggling with their children, a tidy home that could withstand the strictest white-glove inspection, and a fresh-baked pie being pulled from the oven. I was certain moms like that existed, but they didn't live in my neighborhood.

My experience thus far as a mom wasn't exactly what I had imagined from my childhood days with my grandma.

Grandma always seemed to have it together. Always full of joy, she was also calm, cool, and collected. Her safe, comfortable home seemed ideal: central air conditioning in the summer, carpet that squished between your toes, Dove soap in the bathroom, Pepperidge Farm Milano cookies, a leisurely stroll down the block after dinner, and nightly, riveting *Murder She Wrote* episodes. Everything seemed so perfect, including my grandma.

So it is no surprise that her example is what first gave me such a compelling desire to be a mom.

After I had my first child at the age of twenty-three, I was smitten with my bundle of joy. I eased through my days without a care in the world. He was the perfect child, and I was sure it had something to do with the great mom he had! Never mind that he was only one month old. I loved being a mom. It was easy.

Then we had number two. She was beautiful, and I now had a little girl to dress up. I can still picture her sleeping so sweetly in her bassinet basket, handmade by a friend especially for my daughter. She slept so peacefully as I took care of our home and our oldest son. I was well on my way to being like my grandma.

And then? Well, as they say, the wheels began to come off! With every pregnancy, the morning sickness seemed to get worse. By the time I had my third child, I was on my fifth pregnancy, with two miscarriages included. I was officially overwhelmed. I tried giving myself pep talks to get me through, but that never lasted long!

Having number four wasn't much different from number three. Before I knew it, I found myself exhausted with four very small children at home and my dream of "easy mothering" thrown out the window. It wasn't easy. Perfect? Not one bit. Who was I kidding? I couldn't come up with a pep talk exciting enough to help me now.

It wasn't that I was ready to run from being a mom. I just needed what every mom needs—the truth about motherhood. I had been hoodwinked. Mothering had seemed so natural, easy, and instinctive, but it wasn't. Not one bit.

We all enter motherhood with our scenarios planned out. Maybe you planned an "all-natural" childbirth, only to beg for an epidural or be forced into a caesarean. I expected breast-feeding to be easy, only to find it so hard I was brought to tears over and over as I struggled to master it. How about toilet training? I vowed to train my toddlers by twenty-four months, until reality hit and I had to succumb to a much easier method of waiting until they were three years old.

Why Should Motherhood Be Any Different?

When you stop and think about it, what in life is truly natural, easy, or instinctive? Sure, there are things we do without thinking, like breathing, but that's about it! We don't come out of the womb hardwired with wisdom and experience. We come into the world as foreigners who have to figure things out as we grow up.

If you are a working mom, you likely have a skill-set that took you a long time to hone. You studied for years, maybe even doing graduate work, to acquire the skills you need to succeed in the marketplace. You certainly didn't wake up one morning having all the tools you needed for your occupation!

Or maybe you are a talented cook. You likely grew up with a parent or grandparent who passed on valuable cooking insights, techniques, ingredients, and recipes. You didn't just step into the kitchen and immediately know how to cut an onion, tenderize chicken, knead dough, or even turn on an oven!

Even for people who have a natural gift or ability, that skill still has to be developed. I was born with an ability to sing, and for as long as I can remember, I was involved in solos, choirs, recitals, and just about everything musical. For years, I took voice lessons. Even through college, I was cultivating a natural ability that God had given me — but it still wasn't easy!

Why would we think motherhood would be any different? Whether you are talking about breast-feeding, potty training, disciplining, cooking, schooling, or scheduling, we don't automatically enter the world as experts in all aspects of motherhood. I wish we did!

Many women are fortunate to grow up with great examples in the home. Others are not so fortunate. Even with a great example, the truth is that watching and doing are two different things! Motherhood, while sometimes natural and instinctive, is never easy. And becoming a wise mother is sometimes downright difficult.

Wisdom Takes Work

The bottom line is that wisdom takes work. I mean, even Jesus, God in the flesh, had to grow in "wisdom and stature" (Luke 2:52). The Bible, especially the book of Proverbs, is not shy about telling us we need to work at gaining life skills.

Written from the perspective of a father passing on wisdom to his son, Proverbs contains godly advice about relationships, speech, hard work, purity, and more. The purpose of the book is not about just getting information; it's about acquiring skills for life — wisdom.

This is exactly the meaning of the Hebrew word for wisdom, *chokmah* — skill. When the tabernacle was being constructed, God commanded "skilled workers" to make garments for the priests (Exodus 35:25–26). One could just as easily translate that phrase "wise workers," Israelites who had honed and developed "wisdom/ skill" for making fine garments. To possess wisdom is not only to have information, it is to be able to rightly use that information. Biblically, wisdom is skilled living.

So when we think about the book of Proverbs, we are being commanded to pursue skill in living. But this skill for living is not something we are born with. Notice for example the following passage:

> My son, if you accept my words
> and store up my commands within you,
> turning your ear to wisdom
> and applying your heart to understanding —
> indeed, if you call out for insight
> and cry aloud for understanding,
> and if you look for it as for silver
> and search for it as for hidden treasure,
> then you will understand the fear of the LORD
> and find the knowledge of God.
>
> (PROVERBS 2:1 – 5)

Take a moment, go back, and read that passage again. This time, pay careful attention to how many "action" words are in the passage — words that are asking you to "do" something. As you read the passage, circle, write down, or highlight the action words.

Throughout this passage, the reader is encouraged to:

- ❀ *Accept* words.
- ❀ *Store up* commands.
- ❀ *Turn* an ear.
- ❀ *Call out* for insight.
- ❀ *Cry aloud* for understanding.
- ❀ *Look/search* for wisdom.

Only when the reader does all of these things will she "understand the fear of the LORD and find the knowledge of God" (verse 5).

Worth noting is that though wisdom takes work, it also comes with a promise. Verses 7 – 15 describe the different ways wisdom is a reward. Here are a few of the benefits of pursuing wisdom:

- ❀ Wisdom enables success (verse 7).
- ❀ Wisdom is like a shield (verse 7).
- ❀ Wisdom can guard and protect us (verse 8).
- ❀ Wisdom "saves" us (verses 12 – 15). Godly wisdom provides protection from bad, incorrect, or even sinful counsel from others.

So what does all of this have to do with motherhood? Everything! The point is that we desperately need wisdom for raising our children. We don't automatically know how to do it. We don't always find it easy. Sometimes motherhood is the most frustrating work on the planet! So because we don't come hardwired with wisdom, we have to "do" something about it. We have to actively pursue insight, skill, wisdom, and knowledge for the enormous task of shaping another human being. And when we do, it goes well not only for us but also for our families. Wisdom is worth the work to acquire it.

Now What?

Sitting on our back porch, sandwiched between an old green plastic wagon and our patio furniture, is our youngest daughter's bright pink Barbie bike. Sophia hasn't officially ridden her bike all year. Last summer, she confidently declared her independence from training wheels. I was skeptical she was ready, but we removed the training wheels at her request. A few days later, I looked out the kitchen window to see Sophia, seated on her bike with her tippy toes barely touching the cement, "riding" down the sidewalk. After several more passes, I went outside and offered a few biking tips. Much to my surprise, she resisted my attempt to coach her. She had been watching her friends ride their bikes for several months. How hard could it be? In her mind, this was going to be something she just knew how to do, without practice.

And so now there the bike sits—a testimony to how riding a bike is not as easy or natural as it looks. Looking at Sophia's bike, I couldn't help but make the connection with our myth that motherhood is always natural, easy, and instinctive. It certainly isn't, and so we have to take the necessary steps to acquire skill in motherhood. And doing so is a lifelong process.

Okay, so let's get practical. We can all admit by now, hopefully, that we have been hoodwinked to believe motherhood is natural, easy, or instinctive. So what do we do about it? What are some practical steps we can use to knock off this myth and start walking closer to the truth? The following are a few practical and applicable steps to take.

1. ACKNOWLEDGE MOTHERHOOD IS HARD.

Have you ever found yourself in a terrible place as a mom? I have. Unfortunately (for me), it happened at the dentist office.

One day I took all four kids in for a routine cleaning and checkup. After about an hour, the dentist came out to the (very full) waiting room and sat down next to me. In a very concerned and hushed voice, she leaned close and said, "Your daughter has six cavities."

Bella was only six years old. I have never even had a cavity! Now Bella had six cavities? Pretending it was no big deal, I nodded as the dentist went on to explain the process of taking care of these cavities, the many appointments, and the insane amount of money it would cost. Money we did not have at the time.

I held myself together, took a deep breath, and followed her back to the room where my daughter was. There, the dental hygienist, a sweet older woman, sent me a look of profound sympathy. And that is when the tears began to flow. Tears I couldn't stop—even when in profound sympathy the office staff sent me home with a bouquet of flowers!

The downright reality is that motherhood can be plain hard. Sometimes you have no idea why the tears are flowing. Jesus acknowledged this reality when he said, "In this world you will have trouble. But take heart! I have overcome the world" (John 16:33). Jesus gives us reason to rejoice and honor God even in the midst of hard circumstances.

2. ADMIT YOU DON'T KNOW IT ALL AND THAT IT'S OKAY.

As the beginning years of motherhood went by and my mothering skills slowly felt like they were eroding, I secretly pretended I was fine. I failed to admit that I wasn't okay.

Whether you are an expecting mom, new mom, or mom with nearly grown kids, it's okay to admit you don't have all the answers. The hoodwinked mom is quietly and secretly trying to convince herself she knows what she is doing. The hoodwinked mom has not only been fooled by this myth but is also trying to fool others. Just stop—right now!

The Bible calls this second step humility. We need to not only see God for who he is but to see ourselves for who *we* really are. The road to walking out of the dark in this area is to admit we don't have complete knowledge of what it takes to raise children. Take the pressure off of yourself. You have not failed because you don't automatically and instinctively know how to do everything. It takes more courage to just admit you need help.

3. ASK FOR HELP.

Once you admit you need help, the next step is to actually ask for help. Scary, I know! But God has placed us in the body of Christ for a reason. There are likely women around you who are further ahead in years on this journey of motherhood. Maybe these are women who are working moms too. Maybe they are moms who have pre-teens or teenagers. Or maybe they are moms with kids in college or just beyond. One of the best things we can do as we pursue wisdom in motherhood is to seek the counsel of other moms on the journey. There are likely countless women around you who have learned it, been through it, failed at it, or are trying to understand it. We were not meant to walk through motherhood alone.

Also seek out the counsel of trusted doctors, coaches, teachers, or pastors. Many mistakes could be avoided by the simple action of humbly asking someone else for their perspective, advice, or input.

4. COMMIT YOURSELF TO LIFELONG LEARNING.

As you know, motherhood is filled with different seasons. Just when you feel like you have mastered the infant stage, your little bundle of joy turns into a toddler. After the toddler years, your son or daughter starts school, becomes a preteen, then a teenager, and finally a young adult. They don't stop growing, so you shouldn't either!

Over the years, God has blessed me with several older and wiser women. These women have been tremendous voices of truth, encouragement, and support during difficult seasons. These types of relationships are great opportunities to grow. But what is unique about these mentors is that they have helped me grow in different areas and in different ways. It is unusual to find one person who will help you grow in all areas of motherhood. The person you seek out counsel from in parenting may not be the person you seek out advice from in marriage. That's okay! It is more important that you actually pursue godly growth from trusted friends.

Whether we receive advice from friends, books, conferences, doctors, pastors, teachers, or coaches, the important thing to keep in mind is that each new season brings new challenges. We never arrive, so it's important to keep growing. Motherhood is a lifelong process of seeking and gaining wisdom.

Relieving the Pressure

Friends, I don't know what lies you believe about motherhood. I don't know what has you feeling hoodwinked. If you are exhausted, worn out, and desperate for a lifeline, you are in the right place. You are not alone. You are in good company, because not one of us has it all together. You cannot do this alone—you weren't meant to. The idea that motherhood is natural, easy, and instinctive is a myth many of us have believed from the very beginning.

I will be the first to tell you that for many years I silently felt defeated. Nobody would have known it, but on the inside, I carried the weight of thinking something was wrong with the way I was mothering. I thought that because the external reality of motherhood was harder than my internal mothering instincts, something must be amiss. For years I believed the myth that being a mom would be easy. Because I had a longing to be a mom and possessed many natural instincts of motherhood, I wrongly believed the actual task of raising kids would be more natural and easy.

The pressure was relieved by a mentor's compassionate and truthful words. We sat at a table. I was nearly in tears talking about the season we had come out of and where my heart was, when she simply said:

"Motherhood isn't easy. You have to work hard."

When she uttered those words to me, it was so freeing. I don't know why I expected it to be easy. It *is* hard, but it is so, so worth it.

CHAPTER 3

Myth #2: The Way I Mother Is the Right (and Only) Way

Given the choice between being right and being nice, it is better to choose being nice.

—ERNIE HARWELL

Have you heard the term *like-minded* tossed around in certain social circles? The Internet. At church. When referring to friends or coworkers?

It sounds like an innocent enough term, doesn't it? *Like-minded.* It conjures up images of people who like what they believe and also like others who believe just as they do. It seems like a positive thing to have those who share commonality—a band of brothers or group of girlfriends who have the same perspective and support each other.

Yes, being like-minded with others is something we should be pleased with, right? Perhaps. But not when being like-minded transforms into something not so wonderful.

Being "right."

When I (Karen) was first a mom, most of the women I was around at church, and in my circle of friends in my small midwestern town, were strikingly similar in their lifestyles and beliefs. I don't think I tried to do this on purpose; it sort of just happened. Many of the women were already mothers. They lovingly took me under their wings to mentor me. They all seemed to have the same opinions on how they dealt with their pregnancies. Their deliveries. Their mothering of their small—and not-so-small—children. How they viewed marriage. And the Bible. And a woman's role in society and the home. Although I wouldn't say my circle of friends were cookie-cutter replicas of each other, they certainly were very close. And at the time, I loved it.

It felt like a safe place to have my concerns addressed. They were loving and seemed to enjoy sharing advice. And so many of their answers matched each other that I was sure I was getting the best— why, even the "right"—answers to my questions.

And boy, did I have questions! From the moment I first found out I was expecting baby number one, I picked clean the brains of many whom I knew and admired, wanting to know exactly how their homes operated and what their secrets were to raising children who turned out great and godly.

It didn't take me long to develop my own slick little six-step process to magnificent mothering. And my outlook strangely mirrored most of my friends. If I just had a natural birth, breast-fed, and used cloth diapers, made my own baby food, homeschooled, and applied a particular method of discipline, my kids would be as fabulous as all of these women's children seemed to be. And boy, did I want that!

Now please, do not get me wrong. Most of these actions listed above are actually wonderful. Most I would turn to again if another baby came into our home. These methods of mothering are not the problem. The problem is the belief that unless all of them are followed exactly—well, then you aren't *quite* doing it right. That was the posture I quickly assumed. I had my mothering game plan all sketched out and ready to go. And so off I went to childbirth class in preparation for the delivery of our first baby.

Every Monday night for six weeks my husband and I gathered with other expectant parents at the big city hospital as the instructor gave us all sorts of instructions: on how to breathe properly in labor, on what to bring to the hospital when the big day finally arrived, on what to expect the first few weeks at home while caring for a newborn. It was all very exhilarating and valuable.

However, one evening it was our turn as students to do some of the talking. Our teacher gave us a little assignment. We were to answer aloud to the class with our responses to four or five questions. Among the questions were, "Will you return to work after you have the baby? If so, after how long?" "Do you plan to breast-feed or bottle-feed?" And on and on and on.

Oh, my.

One by one the women answered the questions. Almost all of them were returning to work full-time as absolutely soon as they could after delivering. Only a few said they planned to return to work part-time, and none of them were going to stay home and raise their baby without daycare involved. They were all going to use disposable diapers. And if not bottle-feed full-time, they would certainly be switching to the bottle at about a month old when they needed to return to the workforce.

Now, I would like to say that I politely listened to my classmates explain what they planned to do and that I hoped for the best in their situation with their new, sweet babies. However, I did not. A self-righteous and judgmental spirit welled up inside me as I started to run their answers through what I deemed to be the only godly grid possible when raising a child, and in my estimation, these ladies missed the mark—by a mile!

They simply did not fit the rubric I had for a "good mom." And so, when it came my turn to pipe up and give my answers, I did. And rather smugly. Although my palms were sweaty and I was a bit nervous because I really don't like conflict, I felt very passionate about my predetermined mothering plan. And so I rattled off my answers rather nervously, but also in a way that I hoped would make me look better than them by comparison. Why, I even mixed in a little of the old martyr mom for good measure. "Well, we have decided that even though I have a college education and a great job, I will stay home and raise our child full-time so as not to have to put them in daycare all day. I plan to breast-feed and breast-feed only. And use cloth diapers. We are just really looking forward to having this baby and giving it the best life possible."

At least that's what I remember saying. My memory may be shaded a bit because all I can recall was the startled faces of the other women in my classroom. When they gave their answers they didn't mix in any commentary, trying to make others in the class feel bad. They didn't bash women who wanted to stay home or make it seem that bottle-feeding would be better for the baby rather than breast-feeding. They just simply and straightforwardly answered the questions without any spin. If only I had done the same thing!

This was just the beginning of my mental checklist of what was right and wrong when it came to raising children. Whenever I met someone new, in my mind I sized them up as I heard about their life. And so the checking began.

Birth experience — did they have drugs during labor or maybe even a C-section? That would be a check in the wrong column. A check in the right column was someone who had a total earth birth — no drugs, but natural childbirth all the way, baby.

Feeding options? Of course breast is best. I really gave no wiggle room on that one. I could not for the life of me understand why someone would want to stick something artificial in their baby's mouth when they could feed them the way God intended. No exceptions. No grace. (And this strongly held opinion caused me a great deal of humility when, with baby number three, I not only got a horrid breast infection from nursing, but a full-blown breast abscess that forced me to use formula for a month until the condition could be treated and completely cleared up.)

Working outside the home was probably the biggest hot-button issue. We gave up a lot for me to stay home. A second income. Status. Free time for me. (I was a permanent substitute teacher and so I not only got a lunch break but also had one entire planning period off per day where I could go to the teacher's lounge and read a magazine or write letters.) This was probably the area where I was most adamant. I just couldn't think of any good reason that someone would have a baby and then hand them off to someone else to raise.

It never occurred to me that the family might actually need the money to live. Oh, it wasn't that my husband had a lucrative job. He was a youth pastor. We were living on a budget so tight it nearly squeaked. In fact, I not only breast-fed and used cloth diapers because I thought it was good for the baby—and good for the environment—but also because we simply could not afford disposable diapers and formula. I never thought about a possible scenario where a couple might have scaled back all extra expenses possible and still be short on money each month. With our scaling back, we had just enough. And so I assumed others also could do the same—if they really tried.

I had formed heavy-duty attitudes about nutrition as well. No sugar was going to touch my baby's lips. No artificial prepackaged baby food either. Just nurse them until they can eat soft table foods and that was it. Again, this is actually a great plan if you can make it work for your family. But once again I failed to see that not everyone was in my situation and able to have the time to do this. And perhaps not everyone even wanted to!

And so in my mind I continued to check off more boxes of right and wrong.

If you breast-fed, stayed home, and made your own baby food, then check, check, check went the marks in the "right" column. Any other decisions in those three categories earned you three strikes.

These are not the only aspects of raising children over which mothers disagree. There are many more. Should you make your baby sleep in a crib or let them sleep with you? How about the role of a father? Will he be a hands-off dad and leave the diapering and feeding and getting up in the middle of the night all to you, or will he be more of a hands-on father and dive in to also do some of these things to help lighten your load?

Having the premise that there is a right and wrong way to do everything, we seek to discover which way is right. And then once we land there, we can subtly—or even overtly—begin to criticize and even judge others who did not reach the same conclusion as we did.

Something in us just longs to be "right." And perhaps, with some aspects of child rearing, there *is* a right and best way. It isn't like all aspects of child rearing are multiple choice, with each choice being equally beneficial for the child. If faced with the choice of giving a child a needed nap in the afternoon or letting them wander around the neighborhood unsupervised, of course the right thing to do would be to choose the nap! But for many other choices there may be a way that is best for *your* family, *your* child, *your* schedule, or *your* particular situation at the time, but there isn't always a clear-cut, black-and-white, right-or-wrong way.

What does it do to our relationships with other mothers when we assert that there is only one God-approved way to deal with all aspects of parenting? *It makes us erect fences where we could be building bridges instead.*

When we box ourselves in and decide to only be around what we decide are "like-minded mothers," we build a fence—a four-sided fence, actually. Which really in a way is a stinky old pigpen where we shut ourselves up tight inside. Then? Well, we never venture outside those four barbed-wire barriers. We view those on the outside as wrong, or at least misguided. Those on the inside? We identify strongly with them, and our pride can start to rub off on each other.

It's horrifying for me to think about it now, but sometimes I can recall conversations from my like-minded-friends-only days. Especially the way some of us talked about mothers who had a job outside of the home.

Now, first let me say that I loved being a stay-at-home mom. I am grateful to God that we creatively worked out a way for me to be home full-time with our three kids while my husband was a youth pastor and then later worked at a furniture and appliance resale shop.

As I mentioned, we were not rolling in the dough. In fact, we had very little dough to roll up and put into our wallets. I remember looking in the local newspaper once where a grid was listed showing what income levels would qualify for either free or reduced lunches in the public school system. At that time we had no children of school age yet, but if we had, we would have qualified for the reduced lunch price.

But we made it work. We cut corners and clipped coupons and rarely ate out. Vacations were pitching a tent and camping in Grandma and Grandpa's backyard or being blessed with a free weekend at a cottage of a friend with no charge to us. We drove old cars and bought all of our furniture secondhand. But these seemed like small sacrifices for me to be able to be the one caring for our children during the day. So don't mishear me that I've now changed my mind and wish I would've worked outside the home when my kids were small. I don't think I would make that choice today. What I would go back and change is how I thought about—and treated—mothers who did.

But back to the chitchat that went on sometimes in my circle of friends. We weren't very nice. Not at all nice when we talked about women who worked full-time. Sometimes it was rather cryptic and masked with a thin coat of concern for the children. If a child of a full-time working mom acted up at church in the nursery, sometimes a stay-at-home mom would say things like, "Poor thing. She's probably just acting out from being gone from her mom all day" or

"I'm sure she's probably just exhausted. It's impossible to get a good quality nap at a daycare center. If only her mom would choose to stay home with her."

Other times it was overt and not so subtle. Like referring to the brand-new, big house of a working mom at church as the "Shrine to the Working Mom."

Isn't that awful? And really, looking back now, it probably was steeped in jealousy. One-income families aren't usually able to get ahead financially or save money for a down payment or build a bigger home. When it doesn't happen, and we see others around us moving up the financial ladder, sometimes it can breed jealousy. And that jealousy comes out in caustic comments. My sisters, this should not be!

On the other side of the aisle, we have the moms who work outside of the home full- or part-time. Moms in this category face their own set of temptations when it comes to how they view moms who do not bring home a paycheck. Several of my full-time working friends say they sometimes feel jealous of stay-at-home moms. "Must be nice," they think, when they imagine a life without the challenges of getting both the kids and themselves ready to go out the door each morning. They surmise that moms at home have it easy, which sparks feelings of envy. They also tell me honestly that they have looked down on mothers who are at home full-time, thinking they are not contributing members of society, or feeling sorry for them for shelving their intellectual potential and career aspirations to do the menial work of caring for children.

I wish I could say I have never participated in the mommy wars, but I have. While very rarely debating the issue with a member of the other side, I have talked about the other side behind their backs, most often with other members who were on the same side as me. And the funny thing is—now I have been on both sides of this coin! Currently I stand very gingerly on top of the fence, as I am a work-from-home mom of teens and adult children who on most days can be found in my home office, but who also travels away from home to speak at events a few days per month. Thankfully now I have learned to give grace with this issue. But back in the day? Whoa, Nelly!

Today I observe women behaving just like I did back then. And sometimes they unload their opinion on anyone within earshot, whether they are asked to give their opinion or not. In addition, today we have the Internet and social media as avenues where we can sling our opinions.

And the most discouraging and saddest part? Sometimes an overly passionate mom, forgetting that she represents Christ, will hop on her high horse and ride off into battling opinions and jousting at issues. I know I certainly have in the past, and in the mommy wars this ugliness rears its head often.

But Scripture calls us to a higher standard. We are to speak to and about people graciously. Period. In 1 Corinthians 4:12–13 we read, "We work hard with our own hands. When we are cursed, we bless; when we are persecuted, we endure it; when we are slandered, we answer kindly."

We answer kindly.

Hmmm … When Paul was being cursed, he blessed. When he was being persecuted, he endured it. And when he was scandalously slandered, he answered kindly.

Now, having a different opinion about parenting opinions and family lifestyle choices doesn't exactly qualify as being cursed, persecuted, or slandered. We just might feel slightly left out. Somewhat misunderstood. Maybe a little alone. But if Paul says we are to speak kindly even when someone is cursing, persecuting, or slandering us, then certainly we could speak with kindness to someone who has a different opinion than we do on mothering.

Just what does this look like? I'm so glad you asked!

Mommy-er-Than-Thou

Some people crave attention and controversy. They almost like it when there are differing opinions in the room. They may even lean toward being combative, and using their words this way gives them a thrill. I am not such a person. While I certainly have been known to get myself in a tangled-up spat with a member of my immediate family, I don't enjoy verbal sparring with strangers or friends.

However, at times there is tension in the air due to my being on the opposite side of the coin from someone with whom I am speaking. At those times I try to remember the Bible's admonition to speak the truth in love (Ephesians 4:15). And here is another great guideline from Scripture: "Let your conversation be always full of grace" (Colossians 4:6).

Remembering to speak truthfully with grace can help us to temper our tone and package our words in a way that will get across our philosophy without crushing the other person's feelings or making them feel inferior for making a different choice. This is especially true when it comes to other women who are also believers in Christ and desire to follow him.

A Woman's Role in Scripture

So how does all of this disagreement and division rise up in the context of women who all know and love Christ? Part of it can be traced back to certain passages of the Bible.

Titus 2 contains instructions to various groups of people in the church. Here it is in the Amplified Version of the Bible:

> But [as for] you, teach what is fitting *and* becoming to sound (wholesome) doctrine [the character and right living that identify true Christians].
>
> Urge the older men to be temperate, venerable (serious), sensible, self-controlled, and sound in the faith, in the love, and in the steadfastness *and* patience [of Christ].

Bid the older women similarly to be reverent *and* devout in their deportment as becomes those engaged in sacred service, not slanderers or slaves to drink. They are to give good counsel *and* be teachers of what is right *and* noble,

So that they will wisely train the young women to be sane and sober of mind (temperate, disciplined) and to love their husbands and their children,

To be self-controlled, chaste, homemakers, good-natured (kind-hearted), adapting *and* subordinating themselves to their husbands, that the word of God may not be exposed to reproach (blasphemed or discredited).

(vv. 1–5)

See that word *homemakers*? This one little word has caused many an argument when it comes to how women, especially mothers, should be spending their lives.

When this was first written down, it was written in the Greek language. The actual Greek word used here is the adjective *oikour-gos*. This strange-looking word is actually a combo of two other words: *keeper* and *home*. It comes from the word *oikos*, which means "house, household, or family," and *ouros*, which means "a guardian, watcher, warden, or keeper"—all of which carry the meaning of "one who works." So at its very core, the word *oikourgos* (translated in various English Bible versions as "keepers at home," "busy at home," "homemakers," or "managers of the household") carries the meaning of being a working watchman of the home.

We can all agree that these verses say that we must take care of our home and family. But how we will do that is lived out differently for each of us depending on our convictions and life circumstances. You see, we take a modern-day argument (working mom versus stay-at-home mom) and try to apply it to this verse. Today the word *homemaker* means one who is not employed outside the home versus a mom who leaves the house to earn a paycheck. But we also have women who work from their homes and earn money by doing so. Where do they fit in? If stay-at-home moms are obeying this verse, and women who work outside the home are not, then how about the one who works *from* home?

Usually this verse is used by some in the very vocal stay-at-home-motherhood-is-the-only-biblical-way crowd to support their view. Just like Proverbs 31 is used sometimes by full-time working moms to prove that women should work outside the home, since verse 16 shows the woman in this passage buying a field and verse 18 shows that her trading is profitable.

We all want to grab a Scripture to justify our position. Can we all just agree to stop reading into the verse what isn't there and instead focus on what *is* said?

It states that woman is to be busy at home, a keeper of the home who manages it well. Being busy at home means not being idle and lazy. Not lying about on the couch watching TV all day and just letting the family fend for themselves. Not getting sucked into the black hole of Pinterest, pinning away all sorts of delicious-looking recipes and just pointing toward the freezer to the stash of frozen pizzas when our family needs something to eat. So this might suggest that even a stay-at-home mom can be ignoring this verse's instructions by being physically at home but a slacker.

Managing and taking care of your home is something all women must do, whether they work at home, outside of home, or stay at home raising kids full-time. Scripture tells us to nurture and take care of family, making it a priority.

Let's keep the main thing the main thing. Remember, everyone has a different life story. And on some issues of mothering, we ruin friendships—or prevent new ones from forming—when we dig our heels in dogmatically! Such as on the issue of whether a baby should sleep in a crib or with the parents. I've seen heated debates and fractured friendships over this one. Wanna know what I believe? Well ... we had one child who slept with us when he was a baby and two who did not. All three turned out just fine, thank you very much. You know what the issue is for me? Not who is sleeping where ... but *who is sleeping?* If you can sleep with a baby in your bed, and you have a bed big enough to make it safe, then yay! If you can't, don't. Or if you can't get any shut-eye at all with Junior between you and the Mister, then get a crib and a good baby monitor. It isn't who is sleeping where, but where everyone can sleep so the family is the most rested.

Give grace—to others and to yourself! Don't sweat it if you can't make food from scratch like your friend does. Nothing wrong with a good bakery. Don't freak out if you don't grind your own wheat. It's okay. I do happen to grind my own wheat and I love it. But I certainly don't expect everyone else to do the same thing! Just like I pray you don't ask me to make anything with kale. What is up with these moms and kale? I tried it once and it smelled like a giant stink bomb had gone off in my house and no one would touch the stuff. So I will stick to my grinding of wheat. You stick to your munching on the dark, curly green stuff. We will both still love each other, right?

Giving grace helps us judge less when we are sensitive and aware of the unique circumstances that different women face. Giving grace helps us not miss out on opportunities to forge supportive relationships with unlikely—and unlike-minded—people.

I Might Have Missed Her

I hung out with a friend the other day. During our time of sipping lattes at the local coffee house, we caught up on what was happening with each other in our marriages, our mothering, and our homes. It was a delightful time of reconnection for two old friends. And to think I almost missed it.

I don't mean that I was late for my outing with my friend. I mean I almost didn't become friends with her at all. You see, once upon a time we attended the same church. The first day I met her was when I slipped out of the service and into the cry room to nurse my newborn son. She was there also. She was feeding her son who was born at almost the same time as mine, only she was giving him a bottle.

A third woman was plopped in another rocking chair comforting her baby as he slept. The two of them were talking about the fact that the one who was feeding her child formula would be returning to work soon and was grateful that she had found a wonderful woman who was going to stay with her son during the time she worked part-time outside the home in the medical field.

I hate to admit it, but in my mind I wrote off both of these women. I was relatively new to the church and didn't know many women yet, but it didn't take me long to know I didn't want to be friends with either of these. Why, one worked outside the home, and while the other one didn't, she seemed to be supportive of the one who did! In fact, she said she would be praying for her and asking God to work out the daycare arrangement so she could return to work knowing her son was loved and cared for while she was gone.

If God had not convicted me of my judgmental spirit and self-righteous attitude in mothering, I would never have become friends with either of these women. But I am today. I am grateful God humbled me and taught me to stop erecting fences on side issues in Scripture and to start building bridges instead. In fact, the two babies we were feeding that day are both now young adults and productive members of society in the workforce. Her son was bottle-fed and attended public schools. Mine was nursed and homeschooled his entire educational experience.

The point is to make sure that the path you are on is the one God has planned for *you*. Let's stop looking to other women and their choices and look to God instead for direction. Sure, pick other women's brains. Read great books. Observe. Weigh and pray. But make sure that you are going to God and his Word for your mothering marching orders. And then? Go forward with confidence, not condescending cockiness, and serve him and your family as you enjoy your unique journey of motherhood.

CHAPTER 4

Myth #3:
I Am "Just" a Mom

Our lives must find their place in a greater story or
they will find their place in a lesser story.

—STEPHEN SHOEMAKER

"If you ever start working, we can update your information."

Ever start working? I (Ruth) could barely believe my ears, let alone
hold my tongue! I had stopped by the bank to make a deposit and
update our personal information. Things were going great until the
teller asked me for my place of employment. I always struggle when
asked that question.

I run and oversee my own large ministry website.

I am a blogger.

I am a speaker.

I write books.

But . . . I am also a mom.

So sometimes I say I own my own business, sometimes I say I'm a stay-at-home mom, and other times I call myself a "homemaker." This particular time I said "homemaker." This really threw the young twenty-something teller for a loop!

"Is that all you do?" she asked, a bit confused. And then to clarify, she continued, "Okay, so you are *just* a stay-at-home mom?" I heard all of her words, but "just" is what struck me the most. All of the blogs, articles, and talk of being "just a mom" flashed in my mind. I couldn't believe what I was hearing.

"Ummmm, well, I am a *mom*," I stated.

And in the kindest, albeit clueless, tone she replied, "Okay, so that is *all* you do?"

Trying to avoid an unnecessary war of words, and so caught off-guard I didn't know what else to say, I responded with a simple, "Yes, I am a mom." (Probably with a bit of agitation in my tone and an inability to add the word *just* in my response.)

Now, I don't think she meant any ill will toward me in particular or motherhood in general. I really think she was just clearly stating what most of culture views a mom to be. And she said it most pointedly with the word *just*. She had no idea what she was saying, and I was so flabbergasted I didn't really know how to respond.

Regardless of where or how you work as a mom (stay-at-home, work from home, work at home, work outside the home, etc.), it's no surprise to you that our culture's attitude and understanding on mothering has changed. In many positive ways, women are faced with exciting questions. What do I want to do or feel passionate about doing? What *can* I do? What do I feel capable of doing? And what *should* I do? More than a choice, what am I *called* to do? The answers to these questions are not always easily discerned.

One of the struggles many women face when they have children is the feeling of "missing out" on other things. Maybe it is delaying a career choice, educational pursuit, or personal aspiration. Maybe, put another way, a myth that many moms fall into believing is that being a mom is somehow "less than" other pursuits. This can easily leave us moms feeling discouraged, frustrated, or even resentful if we aren't careful to keep our emotions in check.

A fascinating but sobering article appeared in *The Atlantic* several years ago. Entitled "Not Wanting Kids Is Entirely Normal," it was excerpted from the book *Why Have Kids?* by Jessica Valenti. The underlying message of the article was that raising kids was a nuisance. Being a mom wasn't enough; and, if anything, it was an obstacle to greater, more fulfilling pursuits.

In the article, Valenti shares a story about how one mom anonymously commented in a blog about her desire to abandon her child. She had had enough and just couldn't take it anymore. Story after story of women, equally as frustrated and exhausted, began to pour into the conversation thread. For over a year, this post continued to grab the attention of worn-out moms; one mom after another lamented her place in life. The author summarized the emotion of these mothers: "The overwhelming sentiment ... was the feeling of a loss of self, the terrifying reality that their lives had been subsumed into the needs of their child."[1]

For most, the comments would be shocking (seriously shocking!). But the sad and sobering reality is that for a lot of moms, even Christian moms, it can be hard to see the value and worth of motherhood. And the denigration of motherhood can lead a lot of women to question whether or not they even want to be a mom in the first place.

Who Wants to Be a Mom?

When our oldest daughter finished kindergarten, she and her classmates went through a graduation ceremony. There was quite a bit of fanfare surrounding this event, with food, beverages, and an inspiring story time for the students. Each student was publicly recognized with a diploma and even a mini-parade. The parents were outfitted with grins, video cameras, and cell phones. It was a big day for students, and an even bigger day for parents.

Before the conclusion of the ceremony, each student was asked to walk up to the podium and share with the audience what they wanted to be when they grew up. One by one, each student announced his or her desired profession. The list went a little something like this:

"I want to be a teacher."

"I want to be the next American Idol."

"I want to be a firefighter."

"I will play football."

"I am going to be a doctor."

The list wasn't terribly long. I'm not sure anyone in the room really thought (or believed) that the declaration each student was making should be taken seriously. But it was still a proud moment (and really cute I might add). Each goal was a good one, and in many ways, predictable. What was surprising, though, was not what was on the list but what wasn't. Later in the day as I was thinking about the graduation ceremony, it occurred to me that there wasn't one girl in my daughter's kindergarten class who said, "I want to be a mom when I grow up."

I know it's only one class, in one city, in one state, in one corner of the world, so I don't want to exaggerate my observation. It's not my goal to analyze why there weren't more girls in my daughter's class aspiring to be moms when they grew up. My husband and I just found it interesting. I decided then and there that I wanted my daughter to be a mom. Not yet. But some day (like decades from now) I want her to experience the joy (and challenge) of being a mom. I want her to embrace the role of motherhood wholeheartedly. And more than anything, I want her to reject the myth that being a mom is somehow less significant than other pursuits. Because nothing could be further from the truth.

God has set apart the home as his. Home is a place where his presence is to be felt and his purposes are to be pursued. He places parents in those homes as watchmen, pastors, priests, shepherds, teachers, and warriors who have been called and commissioned to pass on their faith to their children for the sake of the world. Motherhood is not an easy mission. But it is God's.

My guess is that most moms struggle, at different times and maybe for different reasons, with the feelings of "just being a mom." The good news is that the Bible is not silent about our significance as moms. There are many examples of important mothers throughout the Bible. One of my favorites is the story of the mother of Moses.

Moses' Mom: Living by Faith

I have always been intrigued by the story of Moses' mother. Far more people know Moses, but his mom, as we'll see, played a critical role in shaping who Moses would become and what he would do. Few stories capture the heart like her story does.

She knew, like every Hebrew woman did at that time, that by Pharaoh's decree she was supposed to throw her newborn boy into the Nile River (Exodus 1:22). However, when this young mother saw how fine her baby was, she hid him for as long she could. But the day came when she had to do the unthinkable. She put him in a basket and pushed him gently off the shore of the Nile. Pharaoh had given the order that all newborn baby boys were to be thrown into the Nile to die. But this young mother put her newborn baby boy into the Nile to *live*. Moses' mom knew who *really* had the power to decide between life and death.

As the story unfolds, Moses' sister, Miriam, watches from a distance as Moses comes ashore in the presence of Pharaoh's daughter. Miriam then approaches her to suggest that a Hebrew woman would be a fitting person to nurse this young, abandoned boy. Upon receiving Pharaoh's daughter's permission, Miriam reunites her baby brother Moses with their mom.

Amazing.

The biblical text doesn't tell us exactly how long Moses' mother nursed him before releasing him back to Pharaoh's palace. What we do know is that Moses grew up to save a nation of fellow Hebrews from slaughter, becoming Israel's great leader and the giver of the Law. One can imagine that though Moses grew up in Egypt, he never forgot where his home was, what it meant, or how it shaped him.

The New Testament gives us further insight into Moses' parents' convictions, conduct, and his character. The writer of Hebrews says it this way:

> By faith Moses' parents hid him for three months after he was
> born, because they saw he was no ordinary child, and they were
> not afraid of the king's edict.
>
> By faith Moses, when he had grown up, refused to be known as the
> son of Pharaoh's daughter. He chose to be mistreated along with
> the people of God rather than to enjoy the fleeting pleasures of sin.
> He regarded disgrace for the sake of Christ as of greater value than
> the treasures of Egypt, because he was looking ahead to his reward.
> By faith he left Egypt, not fearing the king's anger; he persevered
> because he saw him who is invisible.
>
> (HEBREWS 11:23–27)

To witness the providence of God unfold in this story is simply breathtaking. I find myself wanting to jump up and cheer on the sidelines of this narrative. You can't read this story and not see the value of shaping and sending children into the world. God's calling on moms is costly, exhausting, perhaps even dangerous, but it is far from insignificant.

So what can we take away from this biblical story? What does God want to remind you of if you are struggling with this myth of "just" being a mom? Let's take a look at a few applications from this story that will help us in the mothering role that God has called us to.

1. YOUR IDENTITY DOESN'T BEGIN WITH BEING A MOM.

Yep. It's the truth. Your identity doesn't begin with being a mom. This might sound odd since this is a book about motherhood. But as much as God loves and delights in the calling of motherhood, your role as mom is not your core identity. It is certainly part of who you are and what you do, but it is not your primary identity.

When I read the story of the mother of Moses, I am struck with her motivation to be found faithful in God's eyes and not just favored in men's eyes. As we read in Hebrews, she was a woman who was "not afraid of the king's edict." She was one of God's people, chosen to be a different kind of community in the world and for the world. Who she was as a daughter of God informed what she did as a mom.

The desire to be seen in a particular way is a reflection of our need to find our worth or identity. As moms, this has to start with who we are in Christ. Motherhood is a part, but it is not the whole. Rather, the great truth is that our worth and identity are found in Christ. As Colossians 3:3 says, "For you died, and your life is now hidden with Christ in God."

There is a danger in starting with "mom" as our core identity. The Bible makes it clear that we are "in Christ" before we are "in motherhood." First and foremost, we are daughters of God our Father. The apostle John celebrates this fact: "See what great love the Father has lavished on us, that we should be called children of God! And that is what we are!" (1 John 3:1).

So our primary identity is as a child of God, not a mom.

2. MOMS CELEBRATE THE WONDER OF NEW LIFE.

Have you lost sight of the wonder and power of new life? Has the miracle of bringing a child into existence become old news to you? I know, I know, you probably yelled and cried your way through childbirth (what mom doesn't?). But as time goes by, we can forget the very miracle of life that our children are. We can forget how absolutely astounding it is to watch a real live human being, knit together perfectly by God, come forth from our body. As I ponder that, I am reminded that if we're not careful, the extraordinary can become ordinary to us. Even the gift, mystery, and power of bringing children into the world can be lost on us.

Nothing can shock us back into the knowledge of the preciousness of life like the imminence of death. And that's where Moses' mother comes in. When she gave birth, she had death on her mind, for she knew her baby had a death sentence hanging over his head. Yet one look at him told her, "This baby is precious! This life must be saved!"

Moses' mother understood the power of bringing new life into the world. What she saw in her child was not a nuisance or obstacle to her plans and desires, but a child that was "fine" (Exodus 2:2). She celebrated his life so much that she risked her own in order to protect it.

3. Being unseen doesn't mean you are unimportant.

I think it's safe to say that had God chosen not to include the story of Moses' mother in the Bible, we would never know what she did. Her actions would have remained unseen, unknown, and unappreciated by almost everyone. Yet they would not have been unimportant!

One of the challenges of choosing to embrace motherhood is that so much of what we as moms do goes under the radar or is unnoticed. Nobody is handing out bonuses, writing feature articles, building statues, or even offering a simple "thank you" to most of us.

There are certainly enough reasons for us to feel lonely, and therefore, to feel like what we do isn't terribly significant. But Jesus says, "Your Father, who sees what is done in secret, will reward you" (Matthew 6:4). Jesus reminds us that we serve the God who *sees*. The importance of what we do for God is not contingent upon how many *people* see what we do. God measures our faithfulness to him (and our families) the same, whether others see it or not. The promise is that what is done for God, even when nobody notices, is seen and rewarded by him. If we as moms lose sight of this truth, our hearts can quickly drift into feeling alone, unappreciated, or even resentful. Though moms deserve to be, and should be, supported and appreciated, we should not lose sight of whom we are *ultimately* trying to please.

Richard Foster, in his book *Celebration of Discipline*, summarizes this point well:

> Self-righteous service requires external rewards. It needs to know that people see and appreciate the effort. It seeks human applause—with proper religious modesty of course. True service rests contented in hiddenness. It does not fear the lights, and blare of attention, but it does not seek them either. Since it is living out of a new Center of reference, the divine nod of approval is completely sufficient.[2]

Is the "divine nod" of the God who sees enough for you?

4. BEING A MOM REQUIRES CONNECTING YOUR STORY TO GOD'S STORY.

Several years ago my four-year-old son dropped a box of gumballs on our wood floor. As you can imagine, they went everywhere. I called, "Noah, get that one! Hurry, grab that one before it rolls under the couch! There goes another one over there!" Chaos in bite-size gumballs had exploded in our living room. My arms reached and my hands grabbed this way and that way. It was a scattered mess I could not control.

Afterward, as I thought about that silly event, I couldn't help but think about how my life as a mom can feel just like that. Every day I am "chasing gumballs" rolling here, there, and everywhere. Do you ever wonder if all these random, insignificant mothering moments even matter?

But the story of Scripture is that all of the seemingly insignificant, painful, unexpected, and unseen parts of our lives are connected to what God is doing. A baby floating in a basket was God's doing. So was the intimate and ordinary act of Moses' mother breast-feeding her child. In fact, our lives are so important that God watched even as we were gestating in *our* mother's womb, and he cared so much about what would happen to us that "all the days ordained for [us] were written in [his] book before one of them came to be" (Psalm 139:16).

We may not birth or raise a future leader, as Moses' mother did.
Yet our story is still connected to God's great story of salvation and
redemption of his chosen people.

The writer of Revelation gives us a glimpse of how the story ends in
Revelation 19:6–8.

> Then I heard what sounded like a great multitude, like the roar
> of rushing waters and like loud peals of thunder, shouting:
> "Hallelujah!
> For our Lord God Almighty reigns.
> Let us rejoice and be glad
> and give him glory!
> For the wedding of the Lamb has come,
> and his bride has made herself ready.
> Fine linen, bright and clean,
> was given her to wear."

What an amazing day that will be, the day when God's rule finally
extends over all creation. A day when we are dressed in the linen
Jesus has provided—pure and without blemish. In that day, the
praise will be thunderous for the only One who is worthy.

Do you see the significance? You are a part of that story. You are raising children in that unfolding drama. You are on the stage, walking
by faith, seeking God's kingdom, looking forward to a day that is full
of hope. Your story must be lived in light of the greater story, or you
will never fully understand the significance of your calling!

Friends, we have the best "job" in the world, and we must not un-
derestimate the calling on our lives just because what we do often
goes unnoticed. God is watching. And *he* notices.

CHAPTER 5

Myth #4: Motherhood Is All-Consuming and All-Fulfilling

The human heart takes good things like a successful career, love, material possessions, even family, and turns them into ultimate things. Our hearts deify them as the center of our lives.

—TIMOTHY KELLER, *COUNTERFEIT GODS*

The flip side of undervaluing motherhood is overvaluing motherhood. On the one hand, we worry that we are "just a mom." On the other hand, we think being a mom should be the most fulfilling, most rewarding, most thrilling thing EVER!

All. The. Time.

After all, isn't being a mother what many of us have dreamed about since we were young girls?

Of course not every little lady plays with dolls or acts out "playing house" with her friends. Some like to climb trees or play baseball or work on fixing their bicycle. I (Karen) was part tomboy and part princess myself. While I loved to wear dresses, I also loved hanging with the neighborhood boys, and I was always up for a rousing game of kickball in our neighbor's backyard. But often a few of my friends and I could be found "playing house," one of my all-time favorite ways to spend a lazy afternoon.

In my imaginary world I was a devoted wife and loving mother. And I didn't just have a baby or two. I had a whole slew of them! In real life, I had only one sibling—a brother who was nearly four years older—and I longed to be part of a humongous family. Like the Bakers down the street. They had ten kids! What fun it was to ride by their house at Christmas time and see all ten glitter-decorated stockings hung in their front picture window. They could host an impromptu basketball game out in their driveway using only people who shared their last name. I was just sure there wasn't any boredom at their house with all of those kids and activity. To me, having a house full of siblings seemed like a continuous party, making for a fabulous life.

Whenever my mind migrated to the future, I pictured myself caring for a family. I would have a pack of darling children. A handsome husband. A quaint house with a kitchen bustling with lots of love and delicious, homemade food. While I did think about a career, it was just an add-on to my main dream of being a mother. A career would be fun but not foremost.

For five years after marriage, I worked as a substitute teacher and a high school coach while my husband was a youth pastor. Our lives were full of kids, though we had none of our own yet. Then? One morning upon rising, I discovered that the stick turned blue and a baby Ehman was headed our way. Yippee!

Well, sort of.

My rose-colored glasses fogged over just a few days after leaving the hospital with our new daughter. I simply was not prepared for how exhausting, time-consuming, emotionally draining, and downright difficult motherhood is! Why didn't anyone tell me this? I had observed other mothers. Read tons of books. Watched television and movies. And, although I did see conflict and troubles from time to time, it seems they all got worked out within the thirty-minute span of a sitcom. Or perhaps mothers I knew in real life just did not let me in on the big picture. From my peering into their lives from afar, I got the impression that they not only loved being a mom all of the time, but that it was the very essence of their whole existence and the place from which they'd drawn the deepest fulfillment. This picture of perfection was shattered for me, however, when baby Mackenzie was on about her tenth day of life.

My pregnancy with her had been difficult. I was hospitalized for hyperemesis, which is just a fancy-pants term for morning sickness that lasts all day long. I got sick every morning and most of the day for almost eight months of my pregnancy. In fact, I got sick on the way to the hospital to deliver her! However, although I had a rocky pregnancy, I was looking forward to smooth sailing as a mother. (Hey! I figured I was owed it!)

Well, nearly twenty-four hours of labor and an emergency C-section later, out popped my pink little bundle of joy. I recovered in the hospital for four days and then was sent home with my new darling dependent. The lilac bush by our front door had bloomed while I was in the hospital. It now greeted us with its sweet fragrance. Kenzie was wearing the sleeper I had worn home from the hospital as a newborn, and she was wrapped in the blanket my husband had been swaddled in the day he went home. (Yes. Both grandmas are half-sentimental/half-hoarder.) It was a lovely start to my mothering gig.

I was on an emotional high. My mom came for the first couple of days to help me out by doing laundry, cleaning, cooking, and watching the baby while I showered or napped. Casseroles came from all directions to feed Todd and me. New-mama me simply rested, rocked, and fed my sweet girl. "This isn't so bad," I thought. No sooner had the thought formed in my mind than, well ... Grandma went home, the casseroles quit coming, and complete exhaustion set in.

One day I found myself all alone in the house. My daughter was not a good sleeper, rarely conking out for more than a twenty-minute catnap here or an hour-long snooze there. This was not what I had expected! I thought babies when they were under a year old took two naps a day—one of a few hours in the morning and then a longer one in the afternoon. But not this kid. And even at night she couldn't stay asleep for more than three or four hours at a stretch.

Now, I had been determined before I ever got pregnant that we were not going to use a pacifier. I had the mistaken notion that moms who used pacifiers were just not doing something right. Pacifiers were unnecessary. A good mom should certainly be able to train her child to self-soothe. But one afternoon, I found myself at the end of my rope, hanging by barely a string of sanity.

The baby had not slept much at all the night before, and I had been up most of the night walking the floor with her, trying to get her to fall back asleep. I also attempted to keep her from waking up my husband in our tiny, barely 900-square-foot home, since he had to be at work early the next morning. So that afternoon, I thought I would catch up on sleep while Kenzie napped. I was certain she would be exhausted from that restless night. But no! It was like someone had given her an IV of straight caffeine. She would not fall asleep but instead fussed and cried. And she kicked and screamed like she had a colossal case of colic.

That afternoon I broke my parental promise. I dug deep into the blue and white plastic bag that had been sent home from the hospital full of helpful pamphlets on nursing, samples of newborn diapers, and other assorted first-time-mom tools. I remembered it contained ... wait for it ... *a pacifier!* I was totally desperate and beyond ready to break my vow to never use one of those things. Sure enough, I found it in the bottom of the bag, still wrapped in its sanitary plastic bag. My fear of being a pacifier-parent was overshadowed by my inherent need for at least a few moments of shut-eye to keep myself from checking back into the hospital—this time for mental and physical exhaustion.

I laid the baby in the antique cradle I was using on loan from a friend. I snugged that oak heirloom up next to the couch so I too could lie down next to it. Then I put my hand through the side slats to hold the pacifier in my child's mouth as she lay on her side. It took a few minutes for her little lips to figure out how to use the thing, but eventually she took it. And she not only took it, she fell asleep! For over four hours! I was now the new poster mom for pacifier use. That yellow contraption made of plastic and silicone kept me from losing my marbles. When my husband returned home from work that evening, he found no warmed-up church casserole waiting for him, but he *did* discover his two favorite girls finally asleep. And neither one was bawling anymore.

When Motherhood Stinks

With that magical pacifier, the exhaustion lessened, yet my disappointment in motherhood increased. It just wasn't fun all the time. Nor fulfilling. Nor picturesque or sentimental and sweet like I had imagined as a young girl or even during pregnancy. Suffice it to say, I soon discovered that there are parts of motherhood that simply stink!

This birthed quite a tension in my heart. Although I wanted to reach out to other experienced mothers for advice and encouragement, my pride kept me from giving the complete picture of what was happening in my miniature house each day with this miniature human being. But a few of my experienced and honest mom friends sensed what was happening. They let their guards down and told me stories of their own early mothering days and asked me how I was coming along. Their reaching out was such a gift to me.

As I listened to these women, who I thought were amazing mothers, share about their own struggles with raising newborns and their feelings of disillusionment, I began to feel that I wasn't alone. Nor was I weird. It simply never occurred to me in my pre-mothering season of life that there would be days when I didn't like being a mom—not one single bit! Days when I wanted to throw in the burp rag. Resign. Turn back the clock to the time when I only had to be responsible for myself, not for the feeding and clothing and diapering of another wriggling tiny one—no matter how cute and cuddly they looked when they finally did fall asleep.

Yes, my friends' words of honesty were a gift. One told how she used to dream of hiring a full-time nanny so she could shop, watch old black-and-white movies, and take a nap! Another admitted that when she brought her newborn home from the adoption agency, it took her over a month to get back into the routine of fitting in a daily shower! Still another opened up about her severe postpartum depression and the medical help she'd received.

These true tales of less-than-perfect mommy moments helped me let go of my mom guilt. Mom guilt is the worst guilt of all. Since we have such idealistic visions of what motherhood will be like—*before* we actually have little people running around our house and ruining not only the looks of our homes but also our sched-ules—mom guilt can cause us to feel shame. And regret. And even, in some cases, remorse. When we are placed in an environment where the myth is perpetuated that motherhood is all-fulfilling, we feel that we have nowhere to go with our frustrations. Surrounding ourselves with other mothers who will share honestly about their feelings, and help us to know that our own feelings are not wrong, is crucial to gaining a healthy perspective of motherhood.

Finding that healthy perspective took me a while. However, with some gut-wrenchingly honest mentoring from a few "I've been there and sometimes still am" mom friends, I was able to learn some truths about this myth of motherhood. Let me share them with you.

First, as my wise friends showcased for me . . .

1. IT IS OKAY TO HAVE FEELINGS OF DISAPPOINTMENT.

Drop the mask. Stop faking that smile. It is not wrong to feel disappointed in motherhood. For some, it isn't what we'd hoped it would be, and the tingly, "isn't he or she the most precious thing?" feelings turn to feelings of "I just want some time to myself!" For others, we have the baby bar set too high, and not being able to pull off having a Pinterest-perfect nursery, a from-scratch meal on the table, a baby that adjusts to our schedule, and a life of work or activity that is barely changed from our life B.C. (before child) can send us spiraling downward with feelings of despair. The truth is, life is full of disappointments, parental and otherwise. Where were we ever promised we'd feel happy 100 percent of the time? Jesus himself said, "In this world you will have trouble" (John 16:33). So why, oh why, are we surprised when troubles come along? We moms aren't immune. The key is knowing where to go with our disappointments—to God—and also making sure we have close friends who will allow us to share our struggles honestly and will then pray with us and point us to the Lord for our answers.

2. JUST BECAUSE YOU DON'T LOVE SOME TASKS OF CHILD REARING DOESN'T MEAN YOU DON'T LOVE YOUR CHILD.

Okay ... this one right here has tripped up many a mom! Kids require care, especially when they are brand-spankin' new. They must be fed, diapered, bathed, and burped. They need their clothes and linens washed, dried, and put away—over and over again. There are groceries to purchase, dishes to do. There are forms to fill out and information to fill in—dozens if not hundreds of times over the course of children's days in your home. When they get older and pursue sports or activities there will be p-l-e-n-t-y of times—let me tell you—when you will find your fanny parked in the soccer bleachers or sitting in the carpool line bored out of your ever-lovin' mind!

Caring for kids is hard work. And it is full of mundane tasks that must be repeated days and years upon end. Just because you don't love these tasks does not mean you don't love your children. *Do not* confuse the two. And see if there are some creative ways you can hire out some of the tasks or swap with a friend. I often traded with a friend and took all of our children to a particular sport because I didn't mind sitting through the practices. In return, she took all the kids to a Wednesday evening program at church, and I got the evening to myself. This helped lessen the time I spent doing motherhood tasks I didn't love. But just so ya know—it is possible to love your kiddos and hate some of the things you must do to care for them.

Now, here is a newsflash:

3. IT IS NORMAL FOR MOMS TO SOMETIMES WANT TO RUN AWAY.

Oh, yes, it is. Once, while chatting with a group of friends, we all admitted that we had daydreamed about running away. We imagined a life where we weren't responsible for anyone but ourselves! I admitted I could really dig life as a waitress at a diner, living in a retro, big-city, one-bedroom apartment and spending my free time watching reruns of *Gunsmoke*, researching my family tree online, and sipping iced tea. Can you even imagine doing laundry and grocery shopping for only yourself? *[Sigh.]* But, after we all had relayed our non-mom-and-marriage fantasy lives to each other, we quickly added how it wouldn't last long. We'd miss our families after just a few short days and promptly go running back!

4. IF ANOTHER MOTHER TELLS YOU THAT SHE SIMPLY LOVES HER ROLE AS A MOTHER 100 PERCENT OF THE TIME AND NEVER FEELS DISCOURAGED OR DISILLUSIONED, SHE IS NOT TELLING THE TRUTH.

Early in my mothering and homeschooling days, I was around a few women who gave the appearance that they were the epitome of perfection when it came to being a mom. They not only seemed to do it all, but they also seemed to love it all—all of the time. I felt very small compared to these moms. I thought they must have been dipped in some secret sauce that made them content, fulfilled, and energized simply from having little people calling them mom and by spending all their waking hours carrying out the umpteen duties that resulted from this title. It wasn't until years later that I learned the truth. A few had been totally faking it. They actually grew to resent being a mom full-time with no hobbies or interests of their own. Sadly, some women in this boat eventually chucked their families and set out to "find themselves." For most it resulted in affairs and fractured relationships with their kids. Beware of this image of perfection. Seek out mom friends who will share the joys and the frustrations of motherhood openly and honestly with you and who won't try to paint a picture of perfection instead. Which brings us to our next action step ...

5. SURROUND YOURSELF WITH STRAIGHT SHOOTERS WHO WILL ALSO SHOOT UP A PRAYER ON YOUR BEHALF AT A MOMENT'S NOTICE.

Whatever you do, *find these friends!* You need them in your "favorites" contact list on your phone so you can call or text them when you need support or advice. Or especially during those times when you feel you are on the brink of snapping—either emotionally snapping or snapping at a child. You need strong believers who are also moms in your inner circle. I have four moms who, along with me, form a Good Morning Girls group (check out www.goodmorninggirls.org). Our primary reason for connecting each day via a group text message thread is to check in for accountability, letting the group know we have spent time praying and reading the Bible that day. However, we also utilize this group for mothering advice and emergency prayer. I can't imagine doing life without my Good Morning Girls. If you aren't sure where to find such friends, get plugged into a solid church or Christian moms group. Make it a priority to pray that God will lead you to such friends, and then don't stop praying until you find them!

6. DON'T LET YOUR FEELINGS OF FRUSTRATION WITH MOTHERHOOD DRIVE YOU CRAZY, BUT RATHER STRAIGHT TO YOUR KNEES.

As much as praying friends are important, it is even more crucial that we be praying ourselves. Be sure to use the resource in the bonus material section entitled A Mother's Week of Prayer Prompts to help you in this endeavor. You can photocopy it and either tuck it in your Bible or pin it up at home to help you focus when you pray. You can also make a prayer notebook based on this resource.

Sole Identity or Soul Identity?

Not only do we have the mistaken notion that motherhood is all-fulfilling, we also get the impression that it is all-consuming: that if we are a mother who wants our children to turn out well, then we really can't be spending time doing anything other than mothering—ever! Motherhood must be our sole identity!

By now you should have clued into the fact that we do not stand in the camp of either stay-at-home moms or work-away-from-home moms. And actually, there are so many combinations possible today. You and your husband—should you have one—must prayerfully and carefully decide what blend is the one God has for you at this season of life. And you must also be open to reevaluating and adjusting in the future. Many a mom has eaten her words who said, "I will never work outside the home," or the opposite, "I will never be a stay-at-home mom." If you don't delight in the taste of your own words, we suggest you refrain from using "never"! But whatever combo plate works for you, avoid placing all your eggs in the "best wife and mom ever—and only" basket.

This mothering perspective, while on the surface seemingly godly and scriptural, can be a dangerous trap. It is the perspective that says not just that our families are our first and foremost ministry (which is true and healthy), but that they are our *only* ministry, our sole reason for existing. End of story. Full stop. Now, before a few of you throw this book across the room or set off to find your Bible and prove us wrong, let me explain.

I am a wife. I am also the mother of three children. I take both of these roles very seriously. Throughout my day of work I remember that I am Mrs. Todd Ehman and the mom of Kenna, Mitch, and Spence. I love to spend time with them, serve them, and come up with creative ways to show them that I love them. However, I am more than a mom. I am a daughter. A sister. A neighbor, friend, and coworker. All of the relationships in my life make up the totality of who I am.

If—oh, I can't even imagine—my husband and children were all killed in a car wreck tomorrow, I would not surmise, "Well, then the Lord might as well take me too. My life is over. Those four people were my only ministry and my only reason for existing." No! All around me I see reasons for existing: my aging parents, the new friend from church, my coworkers with whom I get to serve at Proverbs 31 Ministries, my readers—why, even the grumpy neighbor down the street! All of these souls are "on-purpose people." God has placed them in my life on purpose, for a reason. I have many avenues through which to glorify and serve God. My family is the first avenue, but the street doesn't stop there. God doesn't just give me a sole identity. He gives me a *soul* identity, something much bigger than any of us can grasp.

Some women in the Bible were known for being wives and mothers but also had fulfilling other roles:

- ❀ The *woman in Proverbs 31* was a mom. We are told her children rose up eventually and called her "blessed." But we are also told that she reached out to the poor, transacted business with merchants, turned a profit by selling a field, had a great reputation in her community, and was an employer of female servants. Motherhood wasn't her only gig.
- ❀ The *Shunammite woman* (2 Kings 4) was known for her hospitality to others, namely the prophet Elisha. She was also the mother of two sons. This didn't prevent her from reaching out beyond her own four walls.
- ❀ The *New Testament woman Lydia* (Acts 16) was a dealer in purple cloth from the region of Thyatira. We are told she worshiped God and opened her heart to what the apostle Paul said, and as a result, she and her household were baptized. She also invited Paul and his friends to come to her home. Because she had a household, this suggests she may have been married, if not also a mother.

Yes, being a mom is such a huge part of who you are and what you do, but it is not your sole identity. So, as you navigate your life as a mom, it might be wise to keep in mind the following:

1. REMEMBER, FIRST AND FOREMOST, YOU ARE A DAUGHTER OF THE KING.

When life is over, it all comes down to you and Jesus. You will answer for what you did and did not do in life. You won't answer for others. Keep your role as daughter of the King as most important, and find your soul identity in him.

2. DON'T TRY TO BE MOMMY-ER THAN THOU.

Motherhod isn't a contest. Don't try to one-up the other gal by being "mommy-er than thou." That never ends well. It also prevents honest and healthy relationships from forming with other moms due to jealousy and comparison.

3. RECOGNIZE THE DANGER IN DRAWING YOUR SENSE OF IDENTITY FROM BEING SO-AND-SO'S MOM.

Sure the "proud parent of" bumper stickers and the jerseys with "Tyler's Mom" are fun and encouraging to our kids. Just don't take it too far and tattoo an identity on your heart derived only from whose mom you are. This is misplaced worship.

4. DON'T STUFF WHO YOU ARE AND WHAT YOU ENJOY DOING SO DEEP DOWN INSIDE OF YOU THAT LATER YOU RESENT IT.

Keep interests and hobbies alive, as your schedule and familial responsibilities will allow. This can be through employment outside the home, a home-business endeavor, a volunteer position, or a much-loved pastime. Swapping babysitting with a friend when your kids are young is a great way for both you and your friend to do this regularly and for your kids to have fun with other children.

5. MAKE IT YOUR GOAL TO WORK YOURSELF OUT OF A JOB.

Sometimes when motherhood becomes too all-consuming it is because we have become moms who do too much, raising children who do too little. Make it your goal to work yourself out of a job.

My philosophy is that if a kid can run a gaming controller or work a cell phone, then they can run a washing machine, a dishwasher, and a vacuum. Your kiddos need to pull their own weight around the house. After all, they live there too. Put your feet up and watch them cook or clean, even from a young age. You will not only be working yourself out of a job but teaching them much-needed life skills. Someday your kids' spouses will love and thank you for it!

6. TAKE DELIGHT IN THE PART OF YOU THAT WEARS THE NAMETAG "MOM," BUT REALIZE IT IS NOT A PERMANENT PLACE TO HANG YOUR HAT OF HAPPINESS.

Of course, take pleasure in being a mom. It will bring you delight often. However, true joy comes from serving Jesus. If you hang your hat of happiness on being a mom, you will experience despair during the down times or when your child isn't making good and godly choices. Get your true joy from being a follower of Jesus, not from being the mom of so-and-so.

7. DO NOT BE IDLE ABOUT PREVENTING YOUR CHILD FROM BECOMING AN IDOL.

Beware of making your little (and not-so-little) people into little gods. God is God. Anything or anyone else we put in his place becomes an idol. Even wonderful and righteous relationships can morph into idols if we are not intentional about keeping our priorities and relationships in their proper order.

Live Your Priorities

I'm a visual person. I like to surround my work areas in my home, like my desk in my home office or my kitchen sink, with reminders of my priorities in life. These priorities are the Lord, my husband, my kids, my extended family, and the other people whom God has placed in my life.

In. That. Order.

I have several items displayed: framed pictures of my husband and me from our college days and our wedding day. My favorite snapshot of my kids from when they were little tykes. Bible verses sketched out on sticky notes. A quote from author Elisabeth Elliot: *"The difference is Christ in me. Not me in a different set of circumstances."* But the most important item I possess is an old wooden cross fashioned for me by a neighbor boy using two twigs and some rugged jute twine.

While I love spying my nostalgic mementos as I type away (or put the dishes away), I try to remember that the most significant one is the wooden cross. When I became a follower of Jesus at the age of sixteen, placing my trust in him and the finished work he did on the cross to purchase my salvation, my life was turned upside down. Jesus became my everything, my reason for living, my hope for the future. Sometimes during the craziness that is often motherhood, I can lose sight of this relationship. I can become so busy with family and work, serving God and loving it, that sometimes I forget to simply stop and love the God I serve.

Putting Jesus first doesn't mean we neglect our family or our work. It means that in all of the resulting relationships and situations that come from our many roles, we make pleasing him our chief aim. Your walk with Jesus can make you a better wife. Your walk with Jesus will empower you to be the best worker you can be. Your walk with Jesus will improve your relationships with all the people in your life. And most of all, your walk with Jesus will help you to run the race of motherhood properly, with your eyes riveted on pleasing God, not others. Not even your family.

Know where to fix your focus. Only our relationship with God should be all-consuming. Only our service to him all-fulfilling.

All. The. Time.

CHAPTER 6

Myth #5:
A Good Mother Can
Do It All, All at Once

If evolution really works, how come mothers only have two hands?

— MILTON BERLE

Have you ever watched the performance of a one-man band? That silly character with cymbals and shakers and tambourines strapped on his body? He might even have a brace that holds a harmonica and another one that holds a brass horn. When the one-man band kicks into high gear, he begins to play a song (and sometimes sing!) using all of the instruments almost simultaneously. It is very amusing. Delightful to young children. But here's the thing about the one-man band: you don't see many of them. Why? Well, maybe because they are somewhat a thing of the past, but perhaps also because it takes a great deal of effort to do so many things at once. And perhaps because a one-man band may be amusing to the eye but not all that pleasing to the ear.

At times in my mothering experience, I (Karen) have felt the pressure to be a one-mom band when it comes to all things pertaining to my family. And my church. And my neighborhood. And my extended family. Oh, and don't forget whatever educational system my children were in at the time (I have homeschooled, had one in private education, and most recently one who has attended two different public school districts.)

One fall afternoon nearly a decade ago now, this one-mom band almost came crashing down, taking all of her instruments—and her sanity—with her. And the curious thing about it is what nearly sent me over the edge. It was a simple phone call.

Our home telephone rang on an ordinary weekday afternoon. My husband was working the night shift then, so normally we had our family dinner around one o'clock in the afternoon. All of our children were homeschooled at the time, so this strategy worked well for us to gather and enjoy a meal together before the kids finished up their studies for the afternoon and Dad headed off to work just before suppertime.

I was just standing up to start clearing some of the plates from the table, leaving some for my kids to do as well, when the call came. I set a platter of food down on the counter to answer the phone, taking it into the living room to talk.

After a brief moment or two, I returned to the kitchen. The look on my face told my family something was terribly wrong. My chin started to quiver and my eyes began to well up with tears. Suddenly I burst out crying and quickly bolted out of the room and into the master bedroom, where I flung myself on the bed and began to weep.

My husband and children were obviously concerned. What had happened? Was the phone call about a relative who had been in an accident? Had somebody died? Had there been another national tragedy? (This was shortly after September 11.)

My husband gingerly walked into the bedroom and sat on the edge of the bed. He put his hand on my heaving back as I continue to sob into my pillow. "Karen, what's wrong?" he inquired.

He expected to hear a tale of gloom. A shocking story of an injury or fatality. Perhaps another divorce of a friend or the terminal medical diagnosis of a relative. Instead, he heard his wailing wife gather her composure just long enough to utter through her sniffing and stammering these words:

"Senator Garcia's office called to see if I would bake two dozen cookies for his headquarter's workers to eat during the election return results next Tuesday. And … *[sob, heave, sob, sniff]* I SAID YES!"

I then fell back face-first into my pillow, clutched it tightly, and began to weep uncontrollably.

What in the world?

Now what could make a capable and intelligent woman blubber like a baby at the notion of baking twenty-four cookies? It was because I had allowed my plate to get so full being a wife, mother, church member, neighbor, daughter, and friend that I did not even have enough room left to whip up a batch of snickerdoodles or oatmeal scotchies. And yet I felt the pressure to say yes since I felt it was expected of me.

Many mothers feel the pressure to do it all. We also feel the weight of wanting to appear capable and competent. Additionally, stay-at-home mothers face the added perception that they have oodles of time to do all of these things, since they do not work outside the home. Many people think that being an at-home parent automatically adds forty hours a week of free time to a mom's schedule, so she certainly is capable of baking cookies or being the homeroom mom or single-handedly organizing and implementing the Christmas Tea or Mother's Day banquet at church. (Somehow it never occurs to people that while these women may not be at a job forty hours a week, often many of them are watching their children, and perhaps even other people's children, during those forty hours. And those children make messes and need to be fed, which creates work and dishes and, well … pretty much eats up those hours. At-home moms and working moms alike are very busy.)

The combined perception of others and the pressure I put on myself to want to be liked by everyone and viewed as capable and confident all added up to my tipping point that day. It made a normally calm, cool, and collected woman turn into a wailing banshee at the thought of whipping up a sweet treat for the election workers to eat.

Now, I could have politely declined the invitation to contribute some confections to the senator's campaign, but I didn't. Surely I should be able to add this to my schedule. And certainly, I thought, I just couldn't say no to the voice on the other end of the telephone that day. Why, it was my civic duty! And it was a relatively small task. It should not have sent me over the edge like it did. My little conversation with the campaign worker that day taught me some things about trying to do it all. And how trying to do it all nearly does us moms in!

How Did I Get Here?

Sometimes we attempt to be Superwoman and do waaaay more than we were ever designed to do because we are afraid of disappointing others. It is people-pleasing at its very core. But also, we overestimate the amount of activity we are capable of handling. The number of responsibilities we can successfully juggle. The number of instruments we can keep clamoring and honking and jingling in our one-mom band. Let's break these thought patterns down one at a time. Perhaps we can do a little myth-busting of that fictitious and frustrating character — Supermom.

Oh, you know Supermom, don't you? In fact, you have probably tried to be her a time or two in your life. Or maybe you constantly try to be her every day! At the very least you must have spied this completely out-of-control character in at least one of the circles of women with which you run.

Supermom has super powers. Her super power of domestic cleverness is evident to all. She is able not only to keep her home immaculate, but also to bake and cook from scratch all the meals she sets before her family on the handcrafted table she built over the weekend after seeing a DIY project on her Pinterest board. She uses only the finest organic laundry soap on her children's clothing. Her home is tastefully decorated and looks HGTV-worthy no matter when you drop in. Having her home and food just so for her children is high on her list of parental priorities.

Supermom is also a fantastic manager. She runs a tight ship. No missed doctor appointments or late permission slips for her children's school activities. She makes sure her offspring are shuttled to and from their sports and extracurricular activities on time and never forgets to pack a healthy snack to boot. The home's schedule runs like clockwork, and she makes certain her children are not tardy to anything. This woman could not only run a small country, she could probably do it in her sleep.

While being Supermom to her super children, she doesn't neglect the Mister. She is also a super wife. Of course this is also for the children's benefit, because she wants to create a secure and loving environment for her children, a very noble aspiration! Although sometimes Supermom is super-tired, she must put her fatigue on the back burner in order to be emotionally and physically available for her hubby. And for her children, especially when they are younger and require so much of her bodily strength.

Our heroine must also support the proper outfit for a superhero mom. Her cape is flowing and functional, and she looks ever so slim in her snug leotard, making sure no baby bulge shows on her stomach or teacher flab is wobbling on her upper arms as she goes about her tasks. Got to look good for the Mister. And for the kiddos too. You certainly would not want to disappoint them when they brag about their Supermom to the other munchkins on the playground.

But this "I can do it all" character has a warped viewpoint. First, she believes that she must try to do it all in order to keep up her good standing in the church, community, and workplace—and so others will not only like her, they will also think she is extremely capable and completely competent.

Trying to please others—and also make them not only like us but hold our capabilities in high regard—can be utterly exhausting. When we operate under this mindset, we wear ourselves complete- ly out. What does this look like in the life of a mom? And why, oh why, do we keep on living this way?

What it looks like is being a yes-woman. We get an email from someone at church who needs us to be in charge of a project or an event. We say yes. Now, it might be that we enjoy the responsibil- ities and duties that come with this role, and certainly we should be serving in our local church. But there are times when we say yes just because we feel the pressure from others to do so.

Maybe we have been in charge of this activity or served in this capac- ity in the past, and so we feel obligated to continue. Or maybe we really like the person asking us to assume the duty, and we fear that if we say no, he or she will not like us in return. Or maybe the person who sent the email seems to juggle three or four different roles at church effortlessly, while we aren't really serving beyond showing up for the services each week. We might even feel a little embarrassed saying no to one responsibility when she seems to take on multiple ones with ease. And in the case of the woman who does not work full-time outside the home, well, she sometimes feels a yes is almost expected of her since she is viewed as someone with a lot of extra time on her hands. How in the world can she say no when others who are employed beyond their own four walls are pulling their weight? She doesn't want to look like a do-nothing deadbeat, so she is tempted to say yes to the responsibility in order not to appear lazy.

Trying to impress and please others sure takes the wind out of Supermom's sails (or perhaps just lessens the flapping of her cape in the wind!). But people-pleasing and keeping up a good image with others isn't the only thing that gets her cape in a tangled-up mess. There is something else that lands her in this heap of exhaustion:

our domestic defender of the home front also overestimates her own capabilities and underestimates her time constraints.

Sometimes we mothers let our plates get too full. We continue to pile on more and more things. Outside responsibilities. Inside responsibilities. A commitment here. An activity there. A relationship over here. Our plates get piled higher and higher and higher. Then, when asked to take another responsibility, it never even occurs to us that maybe we need to remove something from our already too-full plates to make room for the new item. Why? Because we Supermoms are so sure that if we just rearrange everything on the plate, somehow we can make it all fit. After all, one of our super talents is multitasking. We are already juggling thirteen balls. That fourteenth ball isn't going to make that much of a difference.

Now I am certainly not trying to beat anyone up for this little phenomenon that occurs in our lives as mothers. We women are strong. Capable. Clever. Competent. Resourceful. These are all extremely helpful traits that assist us in our quest to be good moms. But sometimes these strengths can transform into a weakness because we don't take into account one little thing that we women also have:

Limitations.

What? A woman has limitations? That just cannot be. Isn't one of her super powers that she is flexible and bendable? That she possesses great elasticity and can be stretched further than fellow (cartoon) mother Elastigirl herself?

We have to bust up the notion that we women are without limits, that we are capable of continuing to pile high our plates without their ever giving way. If we don't realize our limitations, we can soon find ourselves not only physically incapable of carrying out all we have said yes to, but also can find ourselves emotionally distraught. Why, we might even burst into tears at the thought of baking two dozen cookies!

The Delegation Decision

Not only have I tended to live life too busy, I have also never been a good delegator. I don't know how that came to be; I only know it to be very true. Whether in my home or outside of it, in a committee or work situation, I want to do it all. Now, it isn't necessarily that I think I know how to do it all; it's more to do with the fact that I want for it all be done *my* way.

When all of my children were elementary age and younger, a friend and I started a ministry we called Mug and Muffin. My friend was the one who allowed us to meet in her home as a small group of moms gathered together once a month. She had to get her house clean and ready. And she was fabulous at this task. She is a gifted woman when it comes to hospitality.

There were many other duties that needed to be done in order to facilitate this group. Someone needed to secure a speaker on a particular topic of motherhood each month. That person also needed to correspond with the speaker, giving her details and logistics for her talk and making sure she had directions to the meeting. Someone else needed to type up and lay out a flyer to send to the fifty or so women on the mailing list. (This was before Facebook or any other type of e-vite, so we did things the old-fashioned way and put flyers in the mail.) Once the flyer was designed, someone needed to take it to the printer, pick the flyers up when they were ready, fold them, and stuff, address, and stamp all of the envelopes. Yet another aspect of this ministry was securing and wrapping door prizes after soliciting them from nearby businesses or purchasing them at the store. Someone also needed to run the meeting each month, introducing the speaker and handing out the door prizes in a clever way.

While all of these duties should have been split up between three or four people, I simply did them all myself. Yes, all of them! Somewhat of a control freak, I wanted to make sure things were done right. By that, I mean that they were done *my* way! In my defense, I had been burned in the past by recruiting help for something, explaining in a detailed way what needed to be done, and then passing it off to the person who volunteered to do it. Only there was one slight problem: they either goofed everything up or forgot to do the chore entirely. Since I was in charge of the bigger project and had handed a small piece off to them, when they didn't come through, it made me look bad. And I don't like to look bad! Plus, I had developed the habit of never delegating and always doing everything myself.

I carried this mindset over into my approach to mothering, doing everything that needed to be done in my home for my husband and kids. But it took me only a few brief years to realize that trying to do it all was not only impractical, it was totally exhausting. Thankfully God intervened and allowed me to learn from experience that I really can't do it all or have it all, at least not all at the same time.

Something had to give. I couldn't juggle more balls than a veteran circus performer without dropping many of them on my toes! While a woman who does not work outside the home might need to destroy the myth that she is "just a mom," and that somehow that is "less than" (been there and dwelt there for over a decade and a half!), those of us who either work outside the home or have many irons in the fire with volunteering or doing ministry must realize that we simply cannot do it all, let alone simultaneously and seamlessly. (This is where I now live most of the time with my writing and speaking ministry.)

By making this observation, I am not saying that if a woman either chooses to work outside the home for a personal reason or must work outside the home for a financial one, her children will therefore not turn out well, or she is somehow not quite enough, and her only right and godly option is to be a stay-at-home mom. I am not saying that at all. What I am saying is that we must make choices and then live with the results of those choices. It is simple logic.

It is impossible to be two places at one time. Therefore, if I am away from home a great deal of time in a full-time job, I may miss some milestones in the development of my child. That doesn't mean I am a bad mom. This is not a sin. This is just reality. And if I must work outside the home for financial or other reasons, I need to trust God in this decision. I cannot beat myself up for not being a stay-at-home mom. I need not fear and fret or spend time worrying that my child will face irreparable damage because I was not home full-time with her.

My mother stayed home with me until I was in the first grade. At that time she became the part-time lunchroom lady at my elementary school, and later, once I entered high school, she worked full-time in retail cosmetic sales. She'd become a single mom when I was in mid-elementary school.

My husband was raised by a mother who was a nurse, and she went back to work full-time the day each of her five children turned six weeks old. Both my husband and I are well-adjusted members of society. We love the Lord. We seek to serve him. Neither of us have needed therapy due to how our mothers spent their days when we were young.

Now if someone wanted to argue from either side of this fence, she could venture off into the subject of research. Oh, you can find convincing research on both sides of this debate. Some state that children are best prepared for life when raised by a mother who stays home. Others conclude that a child adjusts better to society in general if they are placed in a daycare situation early on. Our point in this book is not to debate either side, but to encourage both sides in this: *that God is near and your situation is unique.* He will meet you in the mix of your particular spot. Sure, we need to realize that our choices have natural consequences. We must explore all options carefully before we make our choice—that is, if we have a choice in the matter.

Forget Supermom, Just Be a Super Mom

There is no such thing as a superhero mother. No Supermom. No Wonder Woman. But there are ways to still be a super mom—the best mom you can be for your particular children. Here are eight ways to stop trying to do it all and start learning to be you. After all, we are human beings, not human doings. Maybe if we focused less on what we do and more on who—and whose—we are, we can find that super mom status we are really longing for.

1. Relax

Relax, mom. Don't be so uptight. Stop stressing as you look around at what other mothers are doing and how many things they seem to be accomplishing in their twenty-four hours each day. You don't have to keep frantically racing to replicate someone else's life. Instead, learn to seek and embrace the unique life God has for you at this age and stage of motherhood. Take a deep breath. Pause. Stop stressing. Quit running. Just relax.

2. Reevaluate

Now might be a good time to really reevaluate your schedule to see just where you are overcommitted or where you might be able to carve out some moments of white space. Get alone with a notebook and sketch out your typical week. What commitments do you have inside your home? At work? At church or other civic organizations? Now go back over them and ask yourself if there are any you are participating in that really aren't the best fit for your life right now. If you identify such activities, come up with a plan of action for how you will release yourself from these commitments in order to free more time for your family or for yourself.

3. Relinquish

Let go of your desire to be everywhere at once. Or your tendency to schedule yourself too thin both inside and outside of your home. Accept the fact that you have limitations. That you cannot clone yourself and be two places at one time. The sooner you let go of the notion that you can have it all, all at once, the better. So relinquish.

4. Resolve

Resolve that from now on you will not take on more than you were meant to do. When asked to take on a new responsibility outside of your home, learn to ask yourself a few questions: Is this really my call? Realize that every need is not necessarily your call. Can you also take on the added responsibility of praying for all the details and people that this new project will bring you in contact with? Ask yourself if five years from now you will be glad you took on this responsibility or if you will regret it. And most of all, ask yourself if you are saying yes to the responsibility just to please someone else. You should only be doing it to please God and because you feel that it is his plan for you right now. Take on a task because you feel called, not just because you feel capable.

5. Rest

Learn to build in periods of rest in your week. God's pattern at creation was for us to take one day each week to cease working and really rest. While many of us who are employed do not work on Sundays (or at least have one day off per week we can use as a Sabbath), sometimes we are just as busy on Sundays as we are any other day of the week. Getting caught up on housework. Or shopping. Spending time on the Internet or social media. Consider making Sundays a set-apart day to cease from any type of work and to instead focus on worship and rest.

6. Renew

Beyond just taking one day a week to rest and worship, build some time in for renewal. Renewal of your mind happens when you are involved in studying God's Word both alone and with a group. If you can't find a group to study with at your local church, consider joining our online Bible studies at Proverbs 31 Ministries (prov-erbs31.org). There, thousands of women gather together online to study God's Word and renew our minds.

Also renew your body. Make sure you are taking time to eat healthy. Build in time to exercise and enjoy fresh air when you can. Also be intentional to renew relationships that encourage and strengthen you and build you up in your mothering. We must constantly be renewed so we do not burn out.

7. RELATE

Make sure you have a sounding board of other people in your life who will help you work through the various options and set your schedule accordingly. A trusted friend or two, along with your husband if you have one, can help you see where you are stretched too thin when you can't seem to notice it. Make sure your relationships include such people. Those who will be honest and open and have your best interests at heart. A mom should not be an island. She needs to surround herself with support and life-giving, rather than life-draining, relationships.

8. REVISIT

Be sure to revisit your commitments at least once, if not twice, per year. Hold them up to the Lord. Ask him if there is anything you currently have on your plate that you should remove. Also ask your family. Enlist the opinions of your husband—and your children, if they are old enough—when it comes to how you are spending your time. Perhaps you can't see that an outside commitment is stressing you and messing with family life, but perhaps others who live in your home will notice it. Be open to their feedback. Take their thoughts into account. Make adjustments as needed. (Be sure to check out the yearly inventory in the bonus material section of this book for guidance on just what questions to contemplate.)

No More One-Mom Band

I simply love the harp. I once attended a church where a teenager played it beautifully during the Sunday morning service. I could listen to it for hours! It was soothing and serene, peaceful and precise. The glorious sound that emitted from this single instrument was completely mesmerizing to me.

If I had the choice, I would much prefer to listen to one person play the harp rather than to hear the sounds that emerge from a one-man band. True, it might take a lot of coordination to be a one-man band. And certainly it can be comical at first and quite entertaining. However, over the long haul, I would much rather listen to one skilled harp player strumming a beautiful song on their single instrument than hear the clashing and honking of the side-show character and his clanging contraption.

When we learn to hone in on our calling and clear our too-full plate, we can begin to focus on making beautiful music in our life. This includes how we spend our time both inside the home and with outside commitments. We each have a song to strum. We do not need to simply copy the score that others around us are following. As we take our concerns prayerfully to the Lord, along with our schedules, he will certainly help us to strike the unique balance that is best for us. He can help us to say so long to the striving to be Supermom and help us discover how to mother in our own distinctive way.

CHAPTER 7

Myth #6: Motherhood Is a Rat Race

He said to them, "Come away by yourselves to a remote place and rest for a while." For many people were coming and going, and they did not even have time to eat.

—MARK 6:31 (HCSB)

Do you ever have those days when you feel like you are running in a million different directions?

You wake up in a frenzy. Your night of sleep was more like a few nights out at sea in choppy, turbulent water—hardly calm and hardly restful! Your feet hit the floor running, and your head is spinning and your heart is pounding with all you have to do—or at least are *supposed* to do.

You are rushing to get your child ready for school while desperately trying to figure out where you put the cleats for tonight's soccer practice. Meanwhile, you scramble for any sort of edible item that you can call "breakfast" for yourself, while trying to figure out how you can make your toddler's diaper last just one more hour until you can get to the grocery store to buy more. All this while fielding important but relentless questions from your other children!

"Mom, do you know where my backpack is?"

"I can't find my toothbrush!"

"Mom, can you braid my hair really quick?"

"I forgot to print my report last night. Can you print it for me before we leave?"

"Mom, can you paint my nails?"

And in case you are wondering . . . yes. These are the questions with which I (Ruth) am typically bombarded almost daily.

Maybe your children are older. You find yourself running like a taxi service, or desperately wishing you had an assistant to keep up with the schedules—volleyball, theater, track, etc. College visits? Research scholarships? Really, your life is so full that you are lucky to have dinner on the table! You find yourself at 3:30 p.m. every day just trying to figure out if you have enough in the cupboards to pull together a meal big enough to feed the bottomless stomachs that await!

I get it. I too often want to shriek a long, shrill, and desperate cry for "heeellllppppp!!!" There are so many days when I wish I could just push the pause button on my life—just long enough to catch my breath, reorganize my thoughts, and get back on task and focus. If only it were that easy! All of the rushing here and there gets exhausting and sobering, when you realize that time is short—*really* short.

In all honesty, I have had to admit defeat. Like Karen, I've quickly dispensed with the myth that I can do it all. I've tried and tried to multitask, organize, and put everything in its allotted spot in my life, but no matter how hard I try, it is never enough. I always end up in the same place, trying to reorganize my life all over again in a desperate attempt to feel at rest. Give me a new year and I am like a straight-A student on the first day of school, all determined to pull out my new planner along with new notebooks, new goals, and new plans that are going to help me get it all together *this* year!

Organizing and planning and scheduling are never enough. Ugh! Sound familiar? No wonder we are tempted to shrug it off with another mommy myth: "Motherhood is just a rat race," we sigh. And maybe it is—if we let it become and stay that way.

Missing Out

Here's the thing: in all of our rushing, I fear we are missing out big time. Missing out on the moments God intends for us to delight in and learn from.

Rushing has caused me to miss some of those quiet alone-times when God is speaking to me. I have had to make an intentional effort to focus my time and mind daily on the Lord, to keep in step with the Spirit.

Rushing has made me miss some of the moments when I could have reveled in my children. I have had to make an intentional effort to focus my heart and mind on the four precious little faces that God has planted right in front of me.

I have come to realize that the only way for the best of who I am to pour out to my family and in my ministry is to sloooow down. Make time for the moments of life. Not only do I need to slow down for the sake of God's using the best of me in the places and with the people he has called me to now, but if I am not careful, I can rush my way right out of hearing from God and following his lead.

In *The Best Yes*, Lysa Terkeurst writes,

> I asked the God of the universe to intersect my life with His revelation, then got up from my prayers and forgot to look. Forgot to seek Him. Forgot to keep my heart in tune with His voice and His invitation.

All because of the chaotic rush of my day.

> When all life feels like an urgent rush from one demand to another, we become forgetful. We forget simple things like where we put our car keys or that one crucial ingredient for dinner when we run into the grocery store. But even more disturbing, we forget God.[3]

Just take a look around at your fellow mom-friends and you will see many faces that wear the look of a worn-out mama. We have hurried our way out of the life that is all around us, and in doing so we have hurried our way right out of the will of God. So how do we begin to get a hold of our schedules and our time? How do we take a step toward walking more purposefully, more awake, and more alive? In part, it begins with seeing time as God does.

Time to Take Time Seriously

Time is irreversible. Once it is gone, you can't get it back. So make your time count. If you have been a parent for more than about an hour, then you have probably heard someone say to you, "They are going to grow up fast. Enjoy these years, because the time will fly by." We have all heard it. Frankly, I want to curl up into a ball and cry my eyes out when I even think of how fast my babies are growing up, so I do *not* need the reminder!

As moms, our quickly growing children are walking monuments to the truthfulness of those kinds of statements. These years, made up of tiny seconds and minutes, keep rolling by and seem to gain momentum. When our kids are at baby stage, time crawls. Then just when our toddler starts running around in many different directions and is difficult to catch or hold onto, time becomes equally elusive! Time flies. I know sometimes it doesn't seem like it. There are days or moments that seem to crawl by. But time is definitely moving—and it is moving fast.

The Bible has a lot to say about time. It's interesting that the very first use of the word *holy* in the Bible is in relation to a day—to time. In Genesis 2:3, we read the following: "So God blessed the seventh day and made it holy, because on it God rested from all his work that he had done in creation" (ESV).

God attaches holiness, the set-apartness, to a day. It would be a day of rest set apart *from* work, but more importantly, set apart *for* God. For generations to come, the Israelites would struggle with this work/rest rhythm. While there is a connection to a day in particular, in general the Bible treats time as important, even sacred. It matters. How we use it and spend it matters. So we need to see time for what it is—holy, sacred, set apart, and fleeting. Our view of time will help us to steward it well.

One of my favorite verses about the sacredness of time is Psalm 90:12: "Teach us to number our days, that we may gain a heart of wisdom." The word *wisdom* in Hebrew means "skilled." To have wisdom isn't just to have information. Those who are wise are not just those who have biblical knowledge. To walk in wisdom is to live skillfully. In a culture that often acts and chooses foolishly, a Christian is someone who walks God's path of obedience and faithfulness, living with skill in a scary world.

And here, the psalmist is connecting skilled living with stewarding time. Part of walking in wisdom is being skilled in the stewardship of the days God in his grace has given us. To waste them or mismanage them is to act foolishly and unskillfully. I love that connection!

Like the psalmist, the apostle Paul stressed the importance of stewarding our time. He writes,

> Look carefully then how you walk, not as unwise but as wise, making the best use of the time, because the days are evil. Therefore do not be foolish, but understand what the will of the Lord is.
>
> (EPHESIANS 5:15–17 ESV)

Here is this word *wise* again. God is instructing us that part of the Spirit-filled life extends to how we use time. We are to "make the best use of our time." Oh, but that can be so, so hard ... can't it?

Stewarding Time Well

So what does that look like? How do we invest time in a way that honors God and serves our family well? The following is a list of ways we can skillfully handle the days we have been given.

1. GET REAL WITH YOUR TIME.

By getting real, I mean get realistic! Some days feel like they last thirty-six hours instead of twenty-four. We've probably all felt like our kids are never going to grow up and leave the house. Those exhausting days make us feel like adulthood is an eternity away! And yet, when we get realistic with our time, we begin to see that we don't have nearly as much time as we think. We really do need to number our days as the psalmist instructs, not so we live fearfully, but in an effort to live more faithfully.

So here is a simple exercise. Start with your current age. Then subtract that from eighty-one (this is the current average age of life expectancy for women in the United States). It feels a little strange, but this number gives you an estimate of how many years you have left on planet Earth! Now if you want to know the number of days, just multiply that number by 365.

Let's do one more calculation. This time it's for your children. Take the current age of your child or children. Subtract their age from eighteen (an estimate of when they will leave your home for college or the workforce). Now multiply that number by 365 days. If my calculations are correct I have 16,425 days left of my life and only 4,380 days from today before my youngest leaves home and I have an empty nest. That is sobering, my friend.

We begin to steward our time well when we see with clarity how sacred time is. Our time as a mom is not infinite or limitless. We count our days so we can make them count. Counting our days will help us clarify our mission as moms and live with greater purpose.

2. BEGIN TO LIVE ON PURPOSE.

About four years ago, I met someone in real life whom I had looked up to from a distance. She had already had a profound impact on my life as a mom strictly through her writing, so you can imagine my excitement when I met her in person. I was at a conference where she was speaking, and I had managed to get in touch with her to see if we could meet. To say I was nervous is a bit of an understatement!

I still remember knocking on the door of her hotel room. I was welcomed into a beautiful atmosphere. Yes, it was just a hotel room, but candles glowed, soft music played, and a few dishes of nuts and chocolate were set out for us to snack on. She had pulled the only two chairs in the hotel room next to each other by the window and made it seem as if I was walking into her cozy home. Who was this woman! My soul let out a deep sigh of relief, and I realized that I had forgotten what being at rest really felt like. I had been running full speed ahead for so long that this type of setting was like a welcoming home, an invitation to rest.

As we sat down, with a look of great care and anticipation, she simply asked me to share about myself and how I was doing. Now, not just your casual, "Hey, how's it going?" This was a deep question, "How are *you*? Really, how *are* you?" She went on to ask, "What is it that you want the world to know? Tell me all about your hope and message for moms!" I poured out my heart, and it wasn't long before we realized that we were kindred spirits. Little did I know at the time that this was just the beginning of a beautiful friendship with Sally Clarkson.

Not long after meeting Sally, I was invited into her home with a group of ladies for a leadership intensive. Sally really poured into our personal lives, and we left no stone unturned. The questions we pondered were monumental for me. It was the first time I began to understand how important it is to live with purpose, to know our hearts with wisdom, and to live out of a real sense of calling. I began to see life, my own heart, motherhood, and the time God had given me through a new lens.

Little did I know that my ministry would grow so rapidly over the next few years, and I would need someone to bring me back to center, to help me sort through all of the good things so I could make time for the best things. Over the last three years, I have taken time every year to revisit these questions and take an inventory of my life over the previous year. I have asked God to show me what it means to *really* live a biblically purposeful life. I have made an honest assessment of my devotional life, prayer life, emotional health, physical health, and family life (for more on this, see our Yearly Personal Inventory for Moms in the bonus material). This time has helped me sort through the things I needed to let go of and ponder the opportunities God was leading me to grab hold of.

Until this time with Sally, my life had become a lot of running aimlessly. I was burning a lot of energy but was unsure of where I was going. My feeble and shallow attempts at "organizing" my life to help me feel better and bring meaning weren't enough. I needed clarity on God's purpose for me as a mom.

3. Understanding our calling always leads to greater clarity.

So I began mapping out my vision for my life and my family. I took time to think and pray through the things that were the most important to me and to the Lord. From there I wrote down my priorities. Now this might look different for you, but let me give you an example of what I came up with to help you get started.

Here are the top priorities on my list:

- ❀ I want to have daily time alone with the Lord in study and in prayer.
- ❀ I want to help pass along my faith, with my husband, to the next generation.
- ❀ I want to be a loving and encouraging wife.

- ❀ I want to be a fun and loving mom who is intentional and fully present.
- ❀ I want to take care of my home so that it radiates beauty and peace.
- ❀ I want us to eat together as a family.
- ❀ I want to be a family that serves together—a family that loves the world.

Just as it helped me, the Yearly Personal Inventory for Moms assessment tool can help you focus on your life priorities and evaluate where you are and where you need to grow.

Friends, I am asking—just short of begging you (okay, I am really on my hands and knees pleading)—to make the time to establish your goals and priorities every year by taking this assessment. Grab your calendar right now and find a day that you can have all to yourself to get this done. You will be so thankful you did. I wish I could sit down in a cozy little coffee shop and discuss face-to-face all that God shows you through this special time with him, but since that won't work, send me an email or shoot me a tweet, because I would love to hear from you. Truly.

4. PUT YOUR CALLING ON A CALENDAR.

Our calling or purpose is no good if it stays in our heads. It has to come alive and be a real part of our daily life. So we need to put our calling on our calendar. In other words, we need to schedule our time in light of our calling and purpose as a mom. This will enable us to live with the right priorities.

So now that I have written down the most important, nonnegotiable priorities in my life, I can create a schedule. A schedule is always helpful, even if it is followed loosely. A schedule helps me keep the day in order and forces me to be proactive instead of reactive. If I have already mapped out my priorities, along with my schedule, I have a "master plan" to look at when making decisions. I automatically can see if what I am being asked to do will fit into my life and schedule.

When sorting out your schedule, be realistic. As a night owl, I have always been a little envious of you early risers! Although I would love to say I am going to rise at 5 a.m. every morning, the truth is that I work much better at night. So in my schedule, I work late. I schedule around who I am, not someone else. Also, remember you are just writing out a basic, bare-bones schedule for the day. Some call this an "ideal schedule." This won't include everything that gets added in. It is more of a skeleton schedule that you follow (loosely). From this point, you can adjust your schedule for each day depending on what activities you have.

Here is an example of my basic daily schedule to help you get started (remember, yours will be different!):

7 a.m.	Coffee and God Time
8–8:30 a.m.	Kids Up and Going
9 a.m.	School Time
12:30–1 p.m.	Lunch
2–4 p.m.	Free Time/Quiet Time/School Time
5:30 p.m.	Dinner
7 p.m.	Family/God Time
8:30 p.m.	Kids' Bedtime
9 p.m.	Relax/Read/Work
11:30 p.m.	Bedtime

What I particularly love about having a schedule is the routine and rhythm that it brings to life. A family, and particularly children, thrive in an environment where there is rhythm. There is a security and stability that comes with structure. Not only do we need it to stay on mission, but our kids do too.

Our time is a lot like money. If we don't budget our time, we can easily waste it. Create a weekly or monthly schedule. Obviously life happens, but a schedule helps us live more intentionally and with more focus. A schedule allows us to integrate our different roles and activities into daily rhythms. Create your normal or desired week on paper and then make every effort to execute the plan!

5. PROTECT YOUR TIME.

"Okay, if you can't find anyone else, I could be the secretary for the school PTO."

"Yes, my husband and I can lead a small group."

"What? You are going to have a once-a-month girl's night out? Of course I would love to go!"

Does this list sound familiar to you? Yes, yes, yes, sure, yes, okay, yes! Let me ask you, are you tired? My personality draws me to be a part of every opportunity and every need that comes my way. Maybe you can identify. Are you the *yes, sure, okay* mom too?

I want to encourage you today that it is okay to say no. I have had to learn this the hard way. Too many times in the past I said yes and then regretted and dreaded the task or event at hand.

Once we accept the ministry that God has given us at home with our family as our first priority, there is freedom. Every choice has a consequence. Something, or someone, is going to feel the consequence of the activities we say yes and no to.

Learn to say no, even to good things. We live in a culture where the opportunities are endless. Most of the opportunities are good things. But at what cost to your marriage, your kids, or your family as a whole? Are there events, activities, or opportunities that God is calling you to say no to? As you know, motherhood has different seasons. Saying no now doesn't mean forever. Learning to discern the best things from all the good things out there takes wisdom. There is freedom in not saying yes to every single thing that comes your way. You come to realize that in saying no, you are actually saying yes. Saying yes to the ones who need you the most right now.

This is where coming back to your vision or purpose assessment is so critical. Maybe once a year is too long for you. Some leaders and coaches suggest coming back to your purpose statement or life vision once a month. Regardless, as opportunities present themselves, filter your choices through the lens of the calling God has put on your life during this season. Go back to your priorities and schedule before you agree to add anything. Ask yourself questions such as the following:

- ❧ Does this complement or conflict with my mission?
- ❧ What will this cost my family right now?
- ❧ What will this cost my marriage right now?
- ❧ Am I tempted to say yes for fear of someone's disapproval?

Protecting our time requires living on purpose. Remember, not everything we *can* do is something we *should* do. Live on purpose, schedule your time, and work hard to protect the precious days and years you have.

6. DON'T BE STINGY WITH YOUR TIME.

Now this might sound a bit like a contradiction from what I have just said above, but stick with me here. Don't forget, your core identity is not as a mom. It is as a follower of Christ. As a Christian, God has gifted each one of us and called us to serve not just our family but also the church family that the gospel has birthed us into. So as critical as it is to protect our time, we also need to remember that we can be too stingy with our time if we're not careful. Remember, you not only have a ministry *to* your family, but you also have a ministry *as* a family.

I've noticed there is a movement recently among families to pare back and focus inward. While I agree wholeheartedly with being present and intentional within our homes with our children, I also think we need to be careful that we don't swing too far in the other direction. A family can become too stingy or protective of their time.

Life for the Christ follower will be hard. God doesn't give us a pass to avoid serving, giving, and living a life that matters for eternity. We will have to work hard and follow God's call, sometimes even when it isn't easy. God's calling is rarely, if ever, comfortable. So as a family who is seeking to serve Christ's kingdom, we need to be careful of guarding our time at the expense of giving our life away to others. We need to be sensitive to the reality that "our plan" is not always God's plan.

We become stingy with our time when we guard it at the expense of investing it in others. Maybe we no longer serve in our church, invite friends into our home, or reach out to neighbors. We overreact to the busyness of life. We need to be careful that we don't treat our time like sacred property, posting "no trespassing" signs for fear of unwanted intrusions. This misuse of our time prevents us from loving and being loved the way Jesus intended.

As you grow in living life on purpose and saying no to the wrong things, you will better invest your time and gifts where they count the most. In your effort to live wisely with your time, be careful that you don't see time as just yours. God has gifted you with time. Our time is not really *our* time. God gives it to us to steward well for his purpose. So be careful of becoming too stingy with your time! There has to be a balance.

7. BE CAREFUL OF LIVING TOO MUCH IN THE FUTURE.

When we live only for tomorrow, we lose today. The time slips past us, tricking us into thinking it is a means to something better. All of us can be tempted to live too much in the future—thinking of when spring comes, planning our next vacation, or looking for a different job. For many people, the "glory days" aren't the past; they are the future. But better is most often what is right in front of us— our spouse, our children, and our family. Don't miss the obvious!

Parenting happens in real time. Don't miss the moments right in front of your nose. Living in tomorrow only causes us to lose today.

Begin to make each day matter with your children. No matter what season you are in, use your time wisely.

8. Don't be fooled by time.

I love what Frederick Buechner says about time in his book *The Hungering Dark*. He writes, "We are fools if we do not live it [our lives] as fully and bravely and beautifully as we can."[4]

My prayer for you is that you will truly see time as sacred, and as a result, you will learn to number your days.

Count them.

Put your priorities on paper.

And I pray that your calling, as uncomfortable and challenging as it is at times, will be not only crystal clear for you but a deep and abiding conviction.

Don't let these days rush by you. Make them count!

CHAPTER 8

Myth #7: Motherhood Is the Luck of the Draw

Your greatest contribution to the kingdom of God might not be something you do but someone you raise.

—ANDY STANLEY

I (Ruth) was at a restaurant recently with my family when a game near the cashier caught our son's attention. On the counter was a medium-sized, clear plastic container filled with water. Inside were colorful moving levers with different-size "landing pads." The object? Drop a coin of your choosing into the top of the plastic box and win a free meal if the coin landed on the right lever. The pile of coins at the bottom of the container should have been a red flag for me that our chances were not good. But our son locked his eyes on it, and it was game over for me.

So one by one, we began to contribute to the growing mountain of change at the bottom of the container. At least three dollars in change later, I knew we would still pay full price at our next visit. I'm usually a stickler about these games. The answer is usually no.

But for some reason, I let the kids have a try, which led to several more tries, which eventually led to me emptying my purse of all coinage.

By the time one of our children actually "landed" a coin, we probably had exceeded the price of the free meal ticket we received for our next visit. Sure, there was some timing involved, but this was not a game of intention or skill but of sheer luck.

Let's be honest, at times, parenting feels the same. It's sort of a luck-of-the-draw, give-it-your-best-shot, cross-your-fingers-and-hope-for-the-best mentality. Have you ever felt that way? Maybe you've felt like you are not entirely sure what you should be doing or even how to do it. So, for many of us moms, it feels a bit like dropping coins into water, hoping that in time, something we do or say with our kids will connect, hit the mark, or land where we want it.

The good news is that God has not left us moms in the dark. We don't have to parent by chance or stumble through motherhood without guidance. God has called us to do far more than take care of our kids: feeding them, keeping them safe, and raising them into independent adults, meanwhile keeping our fingers crossed that we're doing it right. Motherhood is not the luck of the draw, where we parent by luck and chance and just pray to survive the day. Instead, mothering is a *calling* to *shape* our children. And shaping our children requires intentional action. The kind of action that Eunice displayed when she was raising Timothy.

Learning from Eunice

The example of Timothy's mother Eunice gives us a glimpse of what it looks like to shape our children. Timothy was a young pastor in the important city of Ephesus during the first century. Yet he had grown up in a divided home, with a Jewish mother and a Greek father (Acts 16:1).

Timothy's mother, Eunice, as a Jewish Christian, likely was raised worshiping the God of Abraham, Isaac, and Jacob in the synagogue.

In contrast, his father was a Gentile, most likely paying homage to a variety of Greek deities. Some scholars even believe that Timothy's father died, leaving him to be raised primarily by his mother and grandmother. Somewhere along the line, we know that Timothy's grandmother and mother became devoted followers of Jesus. For Timothy, this changed everything. Like his grandmother and mother, he too would put his faith in Jesus as Messiah.

As he grew older, Timothy would go on to play an important role in the early church. He would serve as a colaborer with the apostle Paul in his missionary efforts. In fact, Paul mentions Timothy in six of his epistles (or letters) and refers to him as his "dearly loved and faithful son in the Lord" (1 Corinthians 4:17 HCSB). Although many scholars believe that Paul led Timothy to Jesus, Paul points out that it was Timothy's grandmother and mother who began the work by shaping Timothy at a young age and teaching him the Bible. In essence, they were planting seed after seed far before Paul reaped the harvest. Though we have very little information about Eunice, what we do have is incredibly important as it relates to being a mother who is a teacher, shaper, and sender. Paul says it this way: "I am reminded of your sincere faith, which first lived in your grandmother Lois and in your mother Eunice and, I am persuaded, now lives in you also" (2 Timothy 1:5).

Paul makes a short but powerful statement, so short and simple that it would be easy to overlook. He simply says Eunice had a "sincere faith." Before she was a teacher to her son, she was first a devoted follower of Jesus. Wow! This kind of faith is always contagious, so contagious that Paul was convinced that the same faith Eunice had as a mom now lived in her son, Timothy. We can't ignore this point! Many parents want their children to become what they themselves are not. If we want our children to be disciples of Jesus, then we must first be parents who are disciples of Jesus. You will pass on what you possess. Paul points out that this was the case with Eunice. She was not trying to pass on a faith to Timothy that she herself did not have.

Eunice was the real deal, but apparently she was also intentionally teaching her faith to her son, Timothy. We know that Timothy was learning the Scriptures from a very young age. Paul makes this observation about Timothy, but ultimately it is commentary on Eunice as a teaching and shaping mom. Notice what Paul says: "But as for you, continue in what you have learned and have become convinced of, because you know those from whom you learned it, and how from infancy you have known the Holy Scriptures, which are able to make you wise for salvation through faith in Christ Jesus" (2 Timothy 3:14–15).

Paul makes some staggering statements in these two short verses. Not only did Timothy learn from his mother's teaching, but Paul says he became "convinced." This was not a complacent, comfortable, channel-changing faith. Timothy's faith, because of his mother's teaching and sincere faith, became a conviction and a calling in his life and ministry. Eunice did not live aimlessly, controlled by the whims of fate or the chance of circumstance. Rather, Eunice lived faithfully, in obedience to the will of God for her life. Eunice was a mom who understood the power of shaping.

The Picture We Paint

Now, I know what you are thinking. "Yeah, that sounds great. I wish I could be like Eunice. But I am tired, and I don't even know where to start." I get it. I really do! It all seems so overwhelming when we look at the big picture of our child becoming a godly, mature, world-changing adult. But let me encourage you to envision shaping your child like an artist paints a picture.

> A canvas.
>
> Many colors.
>
> Countless strokes.
>
> Unique lines.
>
> Shading.
>
> Different brushes.
>
> Always vision.

You, my friend, are the artist who, with God's help, is patiently and persistently shaping a new creation. So much of parenting is like painting that masterpiece. It doesn't happen all at once. There are no overnight successes. Stroke by stroke, we are helping to shape our children into whom God has made them to be. Let's use that illustration as we talk about shaping our children, breaking it down to look at each of those necessary elements.

1. PAINT WITH VISION.

Every artist begins with vision. What do you see? What is it you are trying to create on this blank canvas? Parenting begins with seeing. What is your vision for your children?

Several years ago our oldest son played on a fairly competitive basketball team. One of the boys on our son's team was clearly heading toward professional basketball. He was very good, and as it turns out, his father had played in college. Before one of their first games, his dad gave a pep talk to the team. "Practice makes perfect," he said. "My son does dribbling drills for two hours every single night in the basement."

I am not against sports or working hard. What stuck out to me was that this was a parent who had vision for his son. Unfortunately, the vision centered only on his son becoming a great basketball player.

The truth is, parents have vision for their children.

We want them . . .

> To be "good" kids.
>
> To demonstrate academic excellence.
>
> To be well-cultured.
>
> To land a high-paying job.

The list goes on and on. Parents, whether they realize it or not, are parenting with some kind of vision. That vision drives their priorities and determines what they say yes or no to. But is it God's vision? As parents, our understanding of "the right picture" needs to be more biblically defined than culturally informed.

Eunice was a mom with vision. Her goal was to pass her faith on to young Timothy. She was an artist who not only saw the blank canvas but also what she wanted to paint. What you "see" will influence how you "shape."

Many parents, Christian parents included, can get preoccupied with cranking out the next star athlete, American Idol, academic scholar, or successful businessman or woman. These are great goals, but they aren't necessarily Christian goals. We must be motivated, by God's grace, to help shape our children into loving and following Jesus. Our vision has to be first and foremost set on passing on faith to the next generation.

2. PAINT WITH PERSPECTIVE.

Traffic, traffic, traffic! I had not driven much, and never on a busy four-lane city street. I was beyond afraid! With my instructor seated in the passenger seat and myself the designated driver-in-training, I clutched the steering wheel with a death grip as I tried to merge into the next lane.

Then suddenly I came to a complete, screeching halt in the middle of a sea of cars. And it was not by my doing! My instructor had hit the brakes.

I was watching the cars in the right lane move forward while I was merging over to the left lane where the cars were *not* moving. I was accelerating with the right-lane cars, but I was moving into the left lane. Not a good idea!

Boy, am I glad my instructor was watching out for me, ready to hit the brakes at a moment's notice.

Painting with perspective is a lot like driver's training. You have the wheel, but you are not alone. God is seated right beside you, ready to hit the brakes or take the wheel if need be. If we don't parent with the perspective that God is graciously involved, then we will likely struggle with control, fear, and a sense that it's all up to us.

Let's look again at 2 Timothy 3:14–15. Notice what Paul *doesn't* say in the passage: "But as for you, continue in what you have learned and have become convinced of, because you know those from whom you learned it, and how from infancy you have known the Holy Scriptures, which are able to make you wise for salvation through faith in Christ Jesus."

Paul doesn't say that Eunice's methods, techniques, or teaching saved Timothy. The teaching was a means to a greater end. That end was faith in Jesus. New information alone doesn't save our children. A new birth does. No amount of content, rules, memory verses, or Bible charts will bring about a new birth in the hearts and lives of our children. That is the work of God's Spirit. Paul says that the Bible is able to "make you wise for salvation through faith in Christ Jesus." Eunice's teaching wasn't for the sake of teaching in and of itself. She taught so that young Timothy would find and follow Jesus as Savior. God asks for our faithfulness first and foremost. He asks for our availability and willingness to be used by him, not our perfection as mothers.

As a mom who is shaping, molding, and teaching, there is great peace in knowing that motherhood is not just the luck of the draw. What we do matters, but ultimately *God* is in control. As women who are wired to micromanage, there is complete freedom in trusting that God is the One who gives faith. We don't have to control all of the outcomes. God calls us to be faithful, intentional, and consistent. At the end of the day, he is at work accomplishing his purposes in the lives of our children (whom he's entrusted to us).

Paul here is echoing the words of Jesus in his stern rebuke of the Pharisees: "You study the Scriptures diligently because you think that in them you have eternal life. These are the very Scriptures that testify about me, yet you refuse to come to me to have life" (John 5:39–40).

Jesus is not saying that studying and teaching the Scriptures is bad. He is simply making the observation, as Paul did, that biblical knowledge alone doesn't transform hearts. This perspective must always be at the forefront of our parenting. The gospel must always anchor us and hold us steady in stormy weather or clear skies. Everything we do as moms has to be done with the same grace, patience, and love that was shown to us by our Lord. It was God's grace that saved you, and it will be God's grace that saves your children. So as you parent, paint with the stroke of God's grace. You are not alone.

3. PAINT WITH LOVE.

Not only am I thankful that God is *with* me, I am thankful that God is *for* me. As I think back to my high school years when I first became a Christian, I am so grateful God didn't give up on me. What drew me to God was not rules but his gracious invitation into a relationship. His love drew me to love him in response. This is the heart of the gospel.

In 1 John 4:10 we read, "This is love: not that we loved God, but that he loved us and sent his Son as an atoning sacrifice for our sins."

The gospel informs me that my security as a daughter in Christ is based on Jesus' performance, not my own. In the context of this loving relationship I *want* to live in obedience. Rules may change behavior, but they cannot change the heart.

This is why our children desperately need a relationship and not just a list of rules. They need our love and not just our law. Our children need to know that we will not give up on them and that our love for them is not dependent on their obedience. Like God's love, our love patiently instructs, pursues, and endures. This is how we parent, because this is how God parents us.

I remember the first time I heard my husband whisper these beautiful words to our oldest daughter: "Bella, I will always love you. Nothing you ever do will make me stop loving you."

That simple phrase took my breath away. I was reminded in that moment that we must remember to always tell our children that just as God loves us, we will always love them. God never gives up on us, and we will never give up on them.

The great Baptist evangelist F. B. Meyer illustrated this point perfectly when he said, "The love of God toward you is like the Amazon River flowing down to water a single daisy." God's love is powerful and persistent. It is safe, but it is strong.

Our children are going to sin and stumble along the way. At times, they are going to disappoint us. Inevitably, our children will choose foolishness over wisdom because they are imperfect. They are "not yet adults" who are navigating a brand new world. Like us, they are prone to wander.

Breathe easy. All is not lost if your children are not all that you want them to be yet. Keep praying, keep teaching, keep shaping, keep instructing—and whatever you do, keep on loving! Remind them often that your approval of them is not based on their performance.

One of the great summaries of love in the Bible is in 1 Corinthians 13:4–8. While this is primarily about love and spiritual gifts, the application can be made for how we parent. Notice some of the characteristics of love in this passage:

> Love is patient, love is kind. It does not envy, it does not boast, it is not proud. It does not dishonor others, it is not self-seeking, it is not easily angered, it keeps no record of wrongs. Love does not delight in evil but rejoices with the truth. It always protects, always trusts, always hopes, always perseveres.

> Love never fails.

There are several of these attributes of love that especially stand out to me as a mom.

Love is patient. Loves takes its time. Keep the big picture in mind. God is at work in you just as much as he is at work in your kids.

Love is patient, not pushy. Let your patient love create space for your child to grow and mature.

Love is kind. Love is considerate. It brings warmth to a home, not warfare. Your words, attitudes, and actions should be saturated in kindness. Your kindness, not your harshness, will cultivate a healthy child. Don't be surprised if the behavior from your child is a reflection of your behavior toward them. Ouch!

Love is not self-seeking. Love is about pursuing the best interests of others. Marriage and parenting are like a magnifying glass. They expose our selfishness in glaring ways. God's grace enables us to move toward others in sacrificial love. The paradox in the Christian life is that there is joy in giving of ourselves to others.

Love is not easily angered. Anger often exposes what our hearts really want. We want comfort, orderliness, a little quiet, or perfectly obedient children. When those things become most important to us, we get angry when we are deprived of them. God has placed your children in your life not as obstacles to other pursuits but as opportunities to love and shape.

Love never fails. Love is powerful. It has endurance. Love keeps on keeping on. God's love for us is not here one day and questionable the next. It is constant and consistent. Love your children in a way that communicates you will never give up on them.

4. PAINT WITH INSTRUCTION.

"That's mine."

"No, it's mine!"

"Well, I had it first!"

"Well, it's mine!"

As the voices of two of my children became more exasperated by the moment and tears began to fall, I wanted to just plug my ears and pretend it wasn't happening. "Not another argument. How many times in a day do we have to go through this?" I thought.

Within a few seconds I heard my husband summon everyone to the living room. Down the steps little feet tapped, and pretty soon we were all plopped down on the couch. My husband came into the room, sat down, and began to "investigate." The parties involved explained their sides of the story, both pleading their innocence. Our "peace summit" was not moving in the direction of reconciliation. After a few moments of hearing their stories through lots of tears and discovering what actually happened, my husband pulled out his Bible and read aloud:

> What causes fights and quarrels among you? Don't they come from your desires that battle within you? You desire but do not have, so you kill. You covet but you cannot get what you want, so you quarrel and fight.

> (JAMES 4:1 – 2)

As a family, we began to explore why we fight or argue. "What do you do when you both want something?" my husband asked. "How did you respond? How should you have responded according to God's Word?"

Within just a few minutes the two guilty parties looked each other in the eyes and said a heartfelt, "I'm sorry."

I was so astonished at the quick reconciliation that I am sure my mouth gaped. Sit down with the Bible and talk through it. It was that simple! For the Bible is not just a source to be studied but the very words of God to be lived out. These conversations are fertile soil for the fruit of maturity and wisdom in our children.

I wish I could say we always respond this way! We don't, but we try. When we paint with the stroke of instruction, we are doing far more than just punishing our children. Biblical discipline is instructional, shaping their hearts with God's truth. But the instruction must be done with love.

Painting with the stroke of love doesn't mean you are an overly permissive parent. It doesn't mean you don't have boundaries or expectations. Neglecting instruction does a great disservice to our children. Our children need the loving instruction and correction of a wise parent. Instructing through discipline is an act of love.

I have never met anyone who loves being corrected! But God reminds us that his love motivates him to discipline us: "No discipline seems pleasant at the time, but painful. Later on, however, it produces a harvest of righteousness and peace for those who have been trained by it" (Hebrews 12:11).

As parents, one of the most loving things we can do for our children is to shape them through loving discipline or instruction. But instruction and discipline go deeper than just stopping an argument, getting silence, or changing a bad attitude. Biblical instruction aims at the heart.

In our home, we constantly have to have these "conversations." Sometimes they are conversations we have as a family, but most often it is one-on-one. It's an opportunity to discern what is going on and why. We've found this to be far more effective in not only correcting behavior but also in cultivating a relationship.

Following are a few pieces of those conversations that are helpful for disciplining:

Listen to their hearts. What happened? What made you do that or say that? We are attempting to understand our child, not just correct her. The heart is the root of all sin. So looking at the heart helps me as a parent know what is really ruling my child's heart.

Look at what God's Word says. Instructing from the Bible is not brow beating; it's helping our children see how God wants them to walk in wisdom. Encourage them with God's Word. Give them a vision of the person they can become and what life looks like when we walk in foolishness.

Encourage them. It's not always easy to encourage our child when he has just dropped the ball! It is tempting to heap more guilt and pressure on a child who already knows he has blown it. Encourage with instruction, God's forgiveness, and love.

Pray together. Rarely do we end one of our "conversations" without praying. This is a great opportunity to take the child before God's throne. God's Spirit is at work in them. In prayer, we are acknowledging to God, and our child, that we need him.

In these conversations we will continue to capture our children's hearts. Remember, consistent instruction and discipline don't just happen overnight. Like a painter, it is stroke after stroke. Consistency is critical. These consistent conversations are great opportunities to help our children become rooted in their faith.

5. PAINT TO RELEASE.

Last year, some friends of ours had a daughter who graduated from high school. As we talked at the graduation party, I asked, "So how are you handling this?" I am already emotional at the thought of our kids leaving some day, so I was curious what these parents would say. The mother's response was simple. She said, "I didn't raise them to always stay with us."

There is so much truth in that statement! While it may feel like forever from now when they finally go off to college or move out of the house, that day is coming. Don't let that day of release come with regret. Let it come with the resolve of a parent who has done her part to send the light of Jesus into a dark world.

Long before Eunice began the loving, consistent work of shaping Timothy, she had learned the command handed down from her ancestors. When God gave the law to Moses, he wanted to show them how to be a different kind of people. He wanted them to love and serve him in such a way that all of the nations might know him, the God of Israel. So Moses instructed the Israelite parents:

Hear, O Israel: The LORD our God, the LORD is one. Love the LORD your God with all your heart and with all your soul and with all your strength. These commandments that I give you today are to be on your hearts. Impress them on your children. Talk about them when you sit at home and when you walk along the road, when you lie down and when you get up.

(DEUTERONOMY 6:4−7)

What is the main idea Moses is trying to get across to God's people? Moses is giving families a purpose—to pass on knowledge of his love and his law. While God is the one who gives faith, he works through the faithfulness of parents.

In verse 7, the word *impress* in Hebrew can also mean "to sharpen" like an arrow. What a powerful picture. Motherhood is not just the luck of the draw, where we do what we can and hope for the best. Rather, motherhood is a lifestyle of intentional, artisanal shaping and sharpening. We are not just raising a good kid or a productive citizen. We are not just filling our children with Bible knowledge or book smarts. Instead, we are shaping and sharpening them to be released into the world to serve God and love people.

What a privilege!

CHAPTER 9

Myth #8: Everything Depends on Me

Worry looks around. Guilt looks down.
Fear looks back. Faith looks up.

—Unknown

Maybe I could fake being sick. Or pretend I twisted my ankle. I just have to think of something that will get me out of this!

My panicked thoughts scampered through my mind. I (Karen) remained calm and collected on the outside, but inside I was a mess, my heart beating so wildly I was sure it was visibly rattling the Spring Arbor College cougar mascot on my newly purchased T-shirt.

It was my freshman year of college, and I stood staring at it—a legend I'd heard about since my very first visit to campus. "It" was made of wood and nails. It stood tall and plain in the mid-Michigan countryside, yet it taunted and intimidated me until I thought I'd surely faint.

They called it simply "The Wall."

The legend was also a tradition, one that every single freshman who arrived on campus each autumn must take part in. Every new student who attended SAC must scale the ten-foot beast, assisted only by the members of their twelve-member freshman "core group."

One by one, each group stood to face The Wall, trying to figure out how to get all the members of their team up and over it. On the backside of the wall was a platform, about a quarter of the way down from the top. Once a person was over the top of the wall, they could lower themselves gently and stand solidly on the platform. They then could reach back over the wall and assist their classmates who had yet to experience the thrill of conquering this wooden monster.

Getting the first person over was the hardest, since there was no one already on the other side, planted on the platform, to help to pull them up and over the top. Usually teams chose the tallest, thinnest, and most athletic guy to go first. Others hoisted him up on their shoulders, and then he tried with all his might to pull himself up and topple over to the other side.

Our first teammate made it over in exactly that way. Then, one after another, more freshmen were lifted, hoisted, pushed, or pulled until they made it safely to the other side. I did my part to help others over, but I dreaded taking my turn. I knew I needed to be strategic about this; while it was hardest to get the first person over The Wall, it was nearly as difficult to get the last one over too, since they had no one to help lift them. And so, with about four other people remaining besides me, I took my turn.

I tried to speak positively to myself, "Come on, Karen. You can do this. Focus. Jump high and grab on tight."

I backed up a few feet, took a couple running steps toward the wall, and then leapt upwards toward the top with all of my might, praying all the while someone's strong arm would catch me.

After a brief moment of panic when I thought I'd slide back down the wall in shame, I felt the hand of a teammate grab hold of mine and grip it tightly. With all the might I could muster, I simultaneously tried lifting myself up with my arms while swinging my right foot up as high as I could so a teammate standing on the platform on the other side could grab it. After about three tries, I was finally successful. My teammates then hoisted me up to the top of the wall, and I gingerly set my feet down on the other side. Sweet relief.

Once I was safely over, we worked together to get the remaining members of our team up and over. Our core group had done it! We had scaled The Wall.

Just three and a half short years after I was married, I found out I was expecting our first child. I was excited to be carrying a new life, although I also felt fear as I stared at the massive wall of motherhood that I would now have to scale, mostly because I thought all the weight was on my shoulders to be my child's everything. Caretaker. Provider. Cook. Teacher. Nurse. Social director. Counselor. Coach. And probably something else I hadn't even thought of yet. How in the world was I ever going to be able to do all that?

The Great Wall of Motherhood

When you first found out a little person would soon be calling you "Mom," what kind of emotions darted and danced through your mind? Excitement? Wonder? Elation? I'm sure your head was filled with all sorts of thrilling hopes for motherhood.

But what about the thoughts that were not so delightful? What about the deep, dark places of your heart where you harbored real fears—fear that you wouldn't know exactly what to do. Fear that your child might be born with a birth defect. Would he or she have a learning disability that would be discovered once they entered school? And what about the most dreaded parenting challenge of all—teenage rebellion? Do I have what it takes to be a good mother? Can I do it all? And what will happen if I can't?

We found this common thread of dread running through the very honest responses to our survey of three hundred women. Many of them felt almost paralyzed with fear, not just when they first discovered they were going to be a mom but at each new juncture of motherhood. In a very real sense, these moms feel like *everything* depends on them.

Jenna S. expressed this when it comes to mothering in general: "There are so many voices saying so many different things in this area. It's confusing! And makes me feel like I might screw up my kids."

As we have mentioned before, it is easy to look at what others are doing. We end up comparing our mothering, or usually our kids' behavior, to theirs. This only sets us up for defeat.

Keleigh G. feels this way too. She had this to contribute to the discussion:

> I fear sometimes we are too harsh with our disciplining, but other times I fear it's not enough. Where is the medium?? My sister has nine, yes nine, beautiful, well-behaved children, a spotless home, and never seems to struggle with the things I struggle with; and not any fault of hers, but I feel completely inadequate when I'm around her. I can't get my two children to listen to me half the time, my house looks like it was picked up, shaken upside down, and put back in place. Am I giving my best, or could I find more to give/provide?

And who hasn't had the same line of thinking as survey respondent Bobbi F.? I bet if we're all honest, we'll admit that we have thought this at least once in our mothering: "At each new age/stage, because I've not gone down that road before, I wonder if I'm doing the right thing and pray my girls won't be in therapy twenty years from now for mistakes I've made."

Yes, the pathway of motherhood is paved with many stepping stones. Each new stone we must place our foot upon also brings a new set of fears. So how do we learn not only to face our fears but also thrive in the midst of them? Time for a little arithmetic story problem.

Fear Not

Did you know that the phrases "fear not," "do not be afraid," or some other variation appear in the Bible more than 365 times? I simply love this piece of trivia! Apparently God knew that we would struggle with fear, so he gave us enough verses to read a new one each day!

Some of these "fear not" Scriptures came in handy when I was up against things that caused my heart to fret: College exams. My engagement. Life as a newlywed when my husband and I didn't always get along so well. And boy, when I was pregnant with our first child, I relied heavily on these verses, often quoting them aloud to myself over and over again. It encouraged me to not only see what these snippets of Scripture said but also to whom they were spoken.

One of the first people God reassured was Abraham (known as Abram before God changed his name). Listen in on his interaction with God.

> After this, the word of the LORD came to Abram in a vision:
>
> "Do not be afraid, Abram.
>
> I am your shield,
>
> your very great reward."
>
> But Abram said, "Sovereign Lord, what can you give me since I remain childless and the one who will inherit my estate is Eliezer of Damascus?" And Abram said, "You have given me no children; so a servant in my household will be my heir."
>
> (GENESIS 15:1–3)

So it appears that Abram had a little fatherly fear himself. His fear was that he wouldn't get to be a dad at all, and instead his inheritance would be left to someone who did not share his bloodline. But God met him in the midst of his fear, telling him, "This man will not be your heir, but a son who is your own flesh and blood will be your heir" (Genesis 15:4). In fact, this is the first time in the Bible that we encounter God telling someone to not be fearful—and it had to do with parenting!

In his commentary on this passage, Bible teacher Warren Wiersbe declares,

> God's remedy for Abraham's fear was to remind him who he was: "I am thy shield and thy exceedingly great reward" (Gen. 15:1). God's "I am" is perfectly adequate for man's "I am not." ... Your life is only as big as your faith, and your faith is only as big as your God. If you spend all your time looking at yourself, you will get discouraged, but if you look to God in faith, you will be encouraged.[5]

God's "I am" is perfectly adequate for man's "I am not."

Yes. And amen!

Everything does *not* depend on me. If I look to myself, I will be discouraged and dismayed. But if I look to God, I will receive the strength and encouragement I need to parent my kids to his glory.

We see other men and women of the Bible also needing the "fear not" message from God: Moses, the nation of Israel, Joshua, Elijah, Mary, the shepherds who were told of the birth of Jesus by an angel of the Lord. And these are just a few! The Bible is full of people who were scared and in need of the Lord to tell them not to fear. But my favorite character of all who gets courage from the Lord was a mom, just like you and me, who found herself in a tight spot and was consumed with sorrow and apprehension. That woman's name is Hagar.

Singled Out and Scared

Abraham's family was a bit dysfunctional, much like families today. Impatient for his promised descendant to arrive on the scene through his wife, Sarah (we first meet her as Sarai before God also changes her name), Abraham decides to sleep with his wife's servant Hagar in order to produce an heir. Now, before we jump all over the man about this decision, we need to take note of the fact that it was his wife's bright idea and a common practice in that culture. However, her little scheme didn't turn out so well.

When Hagar discovers she is pregnant, things in Abraham's household turn a tad dramatic. Tension breaks out between the two women, and Sarah complains to her husband about her servant. She feels that Hagar has developed a little attitude toward her mistress. Abraham's advice? "'Your slave is in your hands,' Abram said. 'Do with her whatever you think best.' Then Sarai mistreated Hagar; so she fled from her" (Genesis 16:6).

We catch up to this distressed mother-to-be in the second half of Genesis chapter 16. Not too long after Hagar runs away, God catches up with her.

> The angel of the LORD found Hagar near a spring in the desert; it was the spring that is beside the road to Shur. And he said, "Hagar, slave of Sarai, where have you come from, and where are you going?"
>
> "I'm running away from my mistress Sarai," she answered.
>
> Then the angel of the LORD told her, "Go back to your mistress and submit to her." The angel added, "I will increase your descendants so much that they will be too numerous to count."
>
> (GENESIS 16:7–9)

Hagar returns to her home with Abraham and Sarah. She gives birth to a son named Ishmael. You'd think there'd be a happily-ever-after ending. Not so. More trouble ensues, this time when Ishmael is a teen. He taunts his younger brother Isaac—the son who finally was born to Abraham and Sarah—and then he and his mother are sent away again.

Both times when Hagar was in distress and fleeing, God met her— and her son. The first time that God spoke to her, encouraged her, and directed her back to her home, it had a profound effect on Hagar. Let's revisit the storyline to pick up where we left off:

> She gave this name to the LORD who spoke to her: "You are the God who sees me," for she said, "I have now seen the One who sees me."
>
> (GENESIS 16:13)

The God who sees me.

In Hebrew this is *El Roi* (pronounce El Roy — you know, like the cartoon character George Jetson's son, for those of you old enough to remember him!). Hagar was floored by the fact that she had encountered the God who knows and sees her intimately. Intimacy is a fragile and yet wonderful thing. I have heard intimacy described as "into-me-see." Isn't that revealing? God sees into Hagar — feelings, fears, failures, and all. And he sees into us too.

This is the first time in Scripture that this name for God is used. But it is not a one-time name. It is a name that sticks. God is still the God who continues to see us distraught moms who are sometimes like Hagar — feelings, fears, failures, and all.

When later her son bullies his baby brother, God once again meets Hagar in the wilderness in the midst of her loneliness. Even though Abraham had packed some provisions for her and for their son, they soon run out. She finds herself once again in physical, emotional, and spiritual need.

> When the water in the skin was gone, she put the boy under one of the bushes. Then she went off and sat down about a bowshot away, for she thought, "I cannot watch the boy die." And as she sat there, she began to sob.
>
> God heard the boy crying, and the angel of God called to Hagar from heaven and said to her, "What is the matter, Hagar? Do not be afraid; God has heard the boy crying as he lies there. Lift the boy up and take him by the hand, for I will make him into a great nation."
>
> Then God opened her eyes and she saw a well of water. So she went and filled the skin with water and gave the boy a drink.
>
> God was with the boy as he grew up. He lived in the desert and became an archer.
>
> (GENESIS 21:15–20)

The encounters between Hagar and her God teach us much about the way God deals with us as mothers today, especially as we worry about providing for the many needs of our children. What lessons can we draw out of this woman's story? I see at least three.

1. GOD SEES OUR SITUATION.

Hagar isn't the only mother to whom God has revealed himself as El Roi—the God Who Sees. Sure, he may have shown himself to Hagar in this manner first in history, but he didn't stop there. He still is the God who sees—us.

He sees the fears we harbor in our hearts. Fear that we don't have what it takes to be everything our child may need at any given time. Worry that we may run out of the many things we need to give our child to sustain their very life. God knows these deep fears because he not only created us but also became flesh to live among us. Hebrews 4:14–16 explains this concept to us movingly:

> Therefore, since we have a great high priest who has ascended into heaven, Jesus the Son of God, let us hold firmly to the faith we profess. For we do not have a high priest who is unable to empathize with our weaknesses, but we have one who has been tempted in every way, just as we are—yet he did not sin. Let us then approach God's throne of grace with confidence, so that we may receive mercy and find grace to help us in our time of need.

He understands. We can approach in confidence. We will find mercy and grace just when we most need it.

2. GOD KNOWS THE NEEDS OF OUR CHILDREN.

When Hagar and her son ran out of sustenance, God saw their need. He sent an angel. When he saw his child wandering about with no direction, worried about her future and the future of her son, God met her need in a very tangible way. Not only did he send her emotional comfort in the form of the angel, he also sent physical provision for her and her son. God opened Hagar's eyes and she saw a well. She immediately filled her water container and gave her son a drink. (Isn't that just like a mom? Making sure your child has enough to eat and drink is second nature!)

But God did not just provide a beverage for these two that day and then move on, leaving them to fend for themselves. God was with the boy as he grew up in the wilderness, and Ishmael became an expert archer. God didn't leave Ishmael, despite his having misbehaved. He didn't leave Hagar, forcing her to deal with raising a teenager on her own. He continued to be with both of them as Ishmael grew into a man with an occupation.

3. GOD WILL CONTINUE TO PROVIDE LIVING WATER FOR US IN THE DAYS AHEAD.

Jesus says this about himself when talking to a woman he met at a well one day. We glimpse the story in the gospel of John:

> When a Samaritan woman came to draw water, Jesus said to her, "Will you give me a drink?" (His disciples had gone into the town to buy food.)
>
> The Samaritan woman said to him, "You are a Jew and I am a Samaritan woman. How can you ask me for a drink?" (For Jews do not associate with Samaritans.)
>
> Jesus answered her, "If you knew the gift of God and who it is that asks you for a drink, you would have asked him and he would have given you living water."
>
> "Sir," the woman said, "you have nothing to draw with and the well is deep. Where can you get this living water? Are you greater than our father Jacob, who gave us the well and drank from it himself, as did also his sons and his livestock?"
>
> Jesus answered, "Everyone who drinks this water will be thirsty again, but whoever drinks the water I give them will never thirst. Indeed, the water I give them will become in them a spring of water welling up to eternal life."
>
> (JOHN 4:7–14)

Jesus offers us living water—eternal life through faith in his finished work on the cross. Only through placing our trust in him can we have this life—life to the full. Christ promises to never leave or forsake us. He is with us for the long haul in this calling of motherhood if we will only trust in, rely on, and place our hope in him.

With him we don't need to fear the future—neither our own future nor that of our kids.

From Scared to Sacred

Sometimes it seems too "Goliath" and insurmountable, the great wall of motherhood over which we must scale. We stare at it and wonder if we have what it takes. Our hearts pound. Our minds race. We fear the future—for ourselves and for our children. We worry that we might not be able to be everything to our child, to provide what they need at each juncture of life.

Our knees knock. The clanking and clunking drown out any voice of reason.

But what if we stopped listening to the voice inside our head, the one that fears and frets and worries? What if instead we reached up—and out? Out to other mothers who also have to scale the wall, and up to God, who is waiting to tightly grasp our slipping fingers?

I have prayed for people to enter each of my children's lives who will mentor and mold them and who share the same Christian values that my husband and I do. I learned early on that I cannot be everything to my children. And I know God works through community. He used my mother to be my greatest and most important teacher, but he also used other mentors in my life as I grew up. So I began to pray that God would bring along such people in the lives of my children. He did not disappoint.

It was back when I was parading around with my 1980s hair in college that I first I heard the old African proverb: "It takes a village to raise a child."

My CORE 200 professor, who was from Jamaica, told of the way adults in his homeland all chipped in to teach the children of the neighborhood right and wrong. You needn't worry if the kiddos misbehaved when they were down the street playing. They would be corrected by an adult who had the same views on parenting as you did.

Later on, when I was having babies all through the decade that was the 1990s, First Lady Hillary Clinton used the Jamaican proverb for the title of a book in which she attempted to expound on the idea.

Many people I know were up in arms about this concept, asserting that the ancient proverb had now taken on a new twist and what was really being said was, "It takes a big government to raise a child, so let us show you how it is done. Oh, and by the way, we're gonna raise your taxes to do it."

If that was what was meant, then I don't like the statement either.

However, it has always equally rubbed me the wrong way when parents have asserted, "I can single-handedly raise these kids, providing everything they need to turn out right. I will be their only role model, their only spiritual influence, and their only teacher of anything biblical, practical, or academic. Kids need their parents and no one else, thank you very much."

Both of these extremes make me a bit uneasy. I don't want the government raising my kids. But I'm not interested in a totally solo act either.

So, *does* it take a village to raise a child?

Ever since my firstborn was small, I have prayed for women who would connect with my daughter, inspire her, help draw out her God-given passions and model for her what it means to follow Christ. By the time she was twelve, she had latched onto a few wonderful women with whom she spent much time. She babysat their kids or helped them clean house or taught sign language or English to their homeschooled children.

In the meantime, she was also watching these women parent their kids, relate to their husbands, and serve God.

Later on when Kenna was struggling with an issue as a teen, she'd oftentimes pick up the phone or ask to use the car and head out to spend a little time with one of these women. You know, it never bothered me. While I heard other moms lament about the fact that their daughters weren't "coming to them" or "opening up" when they felt they might be struggling, I instead would ask God to show me my place.

Often my place was on my knees before him but quiet before her.

A wise friend once told me, "Don't always talk to your kids about God. Sometimes instead you gotta talk to God about your kids." So he and I would chat. And many times he'd tell me the same thing: to shut my mouth, make Kenna her favorite snack, and leave her a little note telling her I loved her. No lip-flappin' needed about the current issue at hand.

Looking back now on my nearly twenty-five-year-old daughter's life, I see the way God orchestrated the placement of people in her path who have helped mold and shape her, inspiring her to be more like Jesus.

Women like Ellen. And Julie. And Wendy. And Holly. And Melanie. And Lysa. They all played such a big part in my baby girl's life. While I do still feel that as a parent we are our kids' most important teacher and role model, we are not their *only* one.

And no, it doesn't take a village to raise a child.

It takes a parent, guided by God, and a little help from whomever he sends your child's way.

Just be prayerful.

And careful.

And willing to trust God to draw their hearts to his, even if in the drawing a little detour is needed along the way. Remember, more is caught than is taught. And just *telling* children what is right and wrong, along with all the appropriate biblical backup available, doesn't always work. Sometimes they have to learn lessons the old-fashioned and painfully hard way. Or perhaps at least learn them from someone other than you.

Is it time for you to call in some backup?

Some of the most sacred moments for me as a mom have been when I have seen my child grow spiritually—on their own without input from me—as they learned from other mothers and mentors in life. I cannot be their everything. And do you know why I am glad I cannot be everything to my child? Because if I were a perfect mom—knew all the answers, never steered them wrong, could meet their every emotional, spiritual, and physical need—it would bring about a terrible, awful result.

My children would have no need for God.

And so I am grateful down to the tips of my unpedicured toes that I am an imperfect parent, because it makes my children long for a perfect God.

If we have the faith to reach out and reach up, we can go from being scared to finding the sacred call of motherhood. The sacred confession where we admit we don't know what to do. The sacred space where we pour our hearts out to God and cry, as did Hagar, in a wilderness of wondering and worry. It is here in the depths of despair, or at least in the little pockets of doubt that creep into our day, that we learn to grab hold tightly to God. In admitting that we are not enough, we discover that he is.

He knows what is best for our children when we don't have a clue. He knows how to speak to their hearts when we just stand scream-ing at their faces. Only he knows what friendships may be forged as we reach out to other women who also are at the end of their rope, fearing they have messed their children up for good. God alone can provide the living water that will quench our thirst along the way.

As we drink deep from the Living Well, we will finally find our-selves living well as moms. It might take hundreds of verses dealing with fear to be read over and over again, year after year. But God is faithful. He is ready and willing to help us face the fears that come with bearing the title of "Mom."

Why, he not only gives us those verses that tell us not to be afraid, but he's given us another verse that tells us he will be with us as we attempt this titanic feat—climbing the wall of motherhood:

> You, LORD, keep my lamp burning;
>> my God turns my darkness into light.
> With your help I can advance against a troop;
>> with my God I can scale a wall.
> As for God, his way is perfect:
>> The LORD's word is flawless;
>> he shields all who take refuge in him.
>
> (PSALM 18:28–30)

Yes, moms—with our God, we can scale The Wall.

CHAPTER 10

Myth #9: I Have to Do It All Right, or My Child Will Turn Out Wrong

There is no way to be a perfect mother, and a million ways to be a good one.

—JILL CHURCHILL

Tears ran down his dirt-smudged face. I (Ruth) couldn't see him too well. But I could see him well enough to know he was crying. Really crying.

Standing on the pitcher's mound, this ten-year-old was experiencing more than just a fun game of baseball. Sure, he loved the sport, but a lot more was riding on this game. Like any good game, especially one that is close, lots of cheering and shouting was going on. The tension was as thick as the humidity that summer day.

Then I heard his dad. His voice was booming.

They say a mother knows her child's cry. I think it is equally true that a child knows the voice of his or her parent. Out of all the voices, all the cheering, all the yelling, one voice stood out. Suddenly it made sense to me. The focus. The tears. The pressure. This young boy wasn't pitching to win a game; he was pitching to win his father's approval. Ugh!

No matter how old your children are, no matter what activity they are involved in, you know the kind of parent I am describing. The one who is overly involved to the point that you sense they are living (or reliving) their childhood through their son or daughter. We've probably all cringed at that mom or dad who stood on the sidelines of the soccer game, cheerleading competition, or rehearsal and was overly involved! Maybe you are thinking, "I would *never* do that! How could that father be so foolish?"

Let me suggest to you that every single one of us does this to our children in one form or another, whether we think we are "that" parent or not. Yep. If we are honest, we all struggle with parenting the wrong way. And by the wrong way, I mean with the wrong motivation, perspective, or desires. No matter how appalled I felt that hot summer day at the father yelling at his son, the ugly truth is, I really needed to take the log out of my own eye. Ouch.

The Tension Is Real

We recently did a survey at The Better Mom to see just how many moms struggle with "the wrong way" versus "the right way." Out of over 300 moms surveyed, 90 percent said that they questioned their parenting ability. The tension is real for most moms. There is often this weighty and nagging internal question, "Am I doing it the right way or the wrong way?"

Nicole B. says, "Every day I question the journey I'm on. I question if I'm the right person to raise these kids. I question if I'm totally screwing them up. I question if God made a mistake trusting such a mess like myself for three beautiful children."

Catherine S. says, "I constantly worry in my head that I am doing it all wrong and not training and teaching enough of the right things."

Tabitha C. says, "I know no parent is the perfect parent, but we all seem to want to be the perfect parent. I find myself often wondering more about my ability to parent than just allowing God to take care of things. I have made a lot of mistakes in my life. I am always so fearful my parenting will be one of them and in turn I will mess up my child's life."

The statistics really weren't surprising to me. I mean, how many times have I questioned my own ability? For me, that tension continues to grow as my children get older. So I suspected that would be the response. What is surprising to me though is that most of us feel like our questioning is actually a bad thing. We stop short of learning from the internal tension we feel.

Now, I have heard it said many times that everybody parents differently and there isn't a right way and a wrong way to parent. But maybe, like Keirra K. states, there is another way to look at it. Her response to the survey was a great reminder for me.

Keirra says, "Yes, I question my parenting ability! I have been told a few times, by a few different people, that if you DO worry about it, that must mean you are doing a good job. Because if you didn't worry, than that must mean you don't care. If you do worry, you must care enough to consciously try to make good parenting choices."

Indeed, there is no perfect way to parent, but there are certainly better ways. For some, we parent the wrong way because of fear. For others, it is guilt. And certainly for other moms, we parent to right wrongs, relive memories, or attempt to pass on desires we have but which our children may not share. So how can we discover these parenting flaws within ourselves?

Whose Armor Will They Wear?

I have always loved the story of David and Goliath. This story of the underdog slaying the Philistine giant has given countless listeners the courage to face their "Goliaths" in faith. But the often unnoticed backstory of this battle provides helpful insight into parenting. Don't miss this!

When the story begins, Saul is still the rightful king of Israel, but God has anointed David as his successor. In the verses leading up to David's walking out on the battlefield, we read that Saul (most likely with good intentions) tried to dress David for war:

> Then Saul dressed David in his own tunic. He put a coat of armor on him and a bronze helmet on his head. David fastened on his sword over the tunic and tried walking around, because he was not used to them. "I cannot go in these," he said to Saul, "because I am not used to them." So he took them off. Then he took his staff in his hand, chose five smooth stones from the stream, put them in the pouch of his shepherd's bag and, with his sling in his hand, approached the Philistine.
>
> (1 SAMUEL 17:38–40)

What was David saying when he took off Saul's armor? In part, he was resisting the urge to lead like someone other than himself. Instead of wearing Saul's armor and helmet, he picked up his staff and grabbed his sling. He had to do what worked for *him*. David took off Saul's armor so that he could step into his own.

Oh, I *love* that.

I don't doubt for a second that Saul was trying to be helpful. He was using his armor, his experiences, to help dress David. Saul, with good intentions, was being fueled by what he wanted and not what was really best for David. The problem was that David was a different person.

Whoa.

Do you see the connection there? How many times as moms do we do the *exact* same thing? While this is a story about one king trying to pass on his armor to the king-to-be, the story can certainly be applied to parents raising and shaping kids. If we are not careful, then, like Saul, we can try to dress our kids in armor they weren't meant to wear. Maybe even with good intentions, we can shape our kids in the wrong ways.

We'll look more at the "right way" soon, but for now let's discuss what it looks like to make the mistake of parenting in the wrong way. It takes wisdom, patience, and God's grace to help children grow into unique image bearers of God. Don't let your past experience, personality, or desires get confused or conflict with what God has in store for your children.

Which Way Is the Wrong Way?

Psalm 139 gives us a good place to start. We can pray,

> Search me, God, and know my heart;
> > test me and know my anxious thoughts.
> See if there is any offensive way in me,
> > and lead me in the way everlasting.
>
> (PSALM 139:23–24)

As moms, let's take a look at our own hearts. Let's ask God to search us so we can discern the areas where we may be parenting in the wrong way. Sometimes it is challenging to discern what is going on in our own hearts. So as a way of helping uncover ways we may be parenting the wrong way, here are five questions to ask ourselves.

1. ARE YOU PARENTING OUT OF YOUR DESIRES INSTEAD OF THEIR DESIGN?

One of the ways we can parent the wrong way is by letting our personal desires trump what God designed our children to be. If I am going to avoid parenting the wrong way, then I need to let my children's design win over my desires. By design, I mean the unique interests and passions that our children possess. My child is his own person, with different personalities, passions, and even life experiences. There are no cookie-cutter kids!

When my oldest son was about nine years old, he was picking out a song to download. Now, I *love* music. I have been singing since

I was six years old, which is why this particular situation even mattered to me. As he searched for just the right song, he landed on one I would have never chosen! I wanted him to pick a slow, wor- shipful acoustic song—a song with depth and rich lyrical content, a song that really means something. Maybe Hillsong, Chris Tomlin, or Christy Nockels. But rap? Really? I listened quietly to the lyrics. There wasn't anything bad, but there wasn't anything profound either. I remember fighting the urge to speak up and criticize his choice.

"He's not you, Ruth," I told myself. "His tastes and interests may be different. Don't fight a battle not worth fighting. Oh, and (ahem) he's only nine years old!"

This was such a silly situation for me to get frustrated over, but I think it illustrates how easily our own personal preferences and desires can lead us to parent in the wrong way. I would absolutely love for all my children, as they grow, to sing and love music like I do. But they might not. And I have to be okay with that. We must be careful that our desires don't diminish, interfere, or trump whom God has created our son or daughter to be. We parent the wrong way when we try to shape a child our way instead of God's way.

2. Are you parenting out of fear?

How does fear show up in our parenting?

Perhaps we fear the influence of a secular culture, so we zealously shield our children from any contact with "the world."

Perhaps we fear for their safety or well-being, so we hover over them, not allowing them to explore, fail, or experience natural consequences.

Looking ahead, we fear for the future of our children. We live in an increasingly competitive culture, and we worry that our children will have trouble finding their place in the world or finding jobs to support themselves. This quiet, sometimes even unspoken fear drives us into pushing our kids, loading on the homework, and enlisting them in all kinds of activities for fear that they might not excel if they opt out.

Scott Dannemiller recently wrote a thoughtful article entitled "The One Question Every Parent Should Quit Asking."[6] He pointed out that kids are experiencing less free time, increased time spent doing homework, more time shopping, and an overall increase in anxiety. With countless opportunities, even good ones, kids are more stressed than ever. So in Dannemiller's opinion, every parent needs to stop asking: "What might we miss if we don't take advantage of these opportunities?" As he points out, a parent is often driven by anxious thoughts and fears that their children won't excel academically, socially, or athletically. The push is to get ahead. All of this fear fuels busy schedules, stressed-out kids, and broken budgets.

Now, don't get me wrong; I am not saying we should pull our kids from all extracurricular activities. But we do need to be careful that we are not letting the wrong expectations or motivations drive what we do as a parent. We need to be careful that we are not aiming at the wrong goals for our kids. Our aspirations for our children should be measured against God's Word and not the standards of the world.

Our culture pushes us to have our children running a million miles a minute to be a part of everything so they can be the best they can be. We need to fight against that pressure and be sure we are not parenting out of the fear of what our child will or will not become.

3. ARE YOU PARENTING OUT OF COMPARISON?

She is taking her kids to the movies again?

I wish I could do all those fun crafts with my kids.

Seriously, how do her girls always have their hair all dolled up and the perfect outfit on?

These are just a few of the thoughts that I am ashamed to admit have run through my mind. Most days when I am just struggling to brush my teeth and look presentable, I wonder how on earth so many other moms seem to have it all together. The key word there is *seem*. They "seem" to have it all together. Looks can be deceiving.

Comparison almost always happens with those we are most similar to.

A mom compares herself to another mom. Musicians listen to and look at other musicians. Athletes compare themselves not to a carpenter or salesmen but to athletes. A parent compares their children to another's of the same age or similar grade. We are all guilty of comparing!

We live in an increasingly competitive culture, so comparisons come easy. I stated the comparisons of myself against other moms that run through my mind, but all too often our sin can also tempt us to take our eyes off of our own children and instead judge the progress or performance of someone else's child against our own.

So what is so dangerous about comparing? For starters, comparing can be driven by fear. We've already talked about the danger of fear. The flip side of comparison, though, is pride. A pride that says, "I am doing this right. Look what a great child I am raising." We not only want to measure up, we want our children to be better-than.

But comparison can be deadly in other areas for a parent and a child. Comparison is a thief. It robs a parent of joy, contentment, peace. It robs a child of his or her own uniqueness. God has given us children who have been uniquely created in his image. They are God's "workmanship." When we parent our children by comparison, we are trying to squeeze them into someone else's mold. Uniqueness isn't just about who they will become but who they are right now.

It takes wisdom to slow down when you need to, or push and stretch when necessary. Parenting is a tightrope that requires walking carefully between patience and pushing. No child's timing is the same. So be careful of remaking them not just into your image but the image of someone else.

The apostle Paul once wrote to a church to teach and encourage them, and in doing so he used the metaphor of a father: "For you know that we dealt with each of you as a father deals with his own children, encouraging, comforting and urging you to live lives worthy of God, who calls you into his kingdom and glory" (1 Thessalonians 2:11 – 12).

As moms, we too need to encourage, comfort, and also inspire our children to live lives worthy of God. We too need to reject the comparison that can fuel our insecurity, anxiety, and overprotectiveness. Instead, we need to fan the flame of their gifts, personalities, intellect, and abilities. Our sons and daughters are "fearfully and wonderfully made." Let's encourage them in a way that is consistent with who they are, not who someone else's child is. We need to parent not out of comparison but out of God's wisdom for our child.

4. ARE YOU PARENTING TO REMEDY YOUR PAST?

Several years ago, our family went to a restaurant with friends and enjoyed a night out of burgers and bottomless fries. We departed with cups to go, colored placemats, and balloons. We were tired, stuffed, thankful for a night out, but ready to go to home and go to bed!

As we left the restaurant, our kids spotted a carnival going on in the parking lot. Instantly they all clamored, "Can we go to the carnival?" Wanting to get home and call it a day, we said, "Not this time." We were exhausted and it was bedtime.

One of the older dads who had grown kids said, "Let them go! My parents always said no, and we need to say yes more often!"

Now, he had a point. We certainly don't want to say no all the time. However, this story demonstrates how we can make bad parenting choices when we try to make up for the mistakes our parents made when raising us. Perhaps our parents were overly frugal, so we spend with abandon. Or our parents were overly strict, so we become pushovers. The opposite can also be true: perhaps our parents lived chaotic lives, so we choose to live with military precision.

None of us were parented perfectly, and none of us will parent perfectly. But it can be dangerous to parent in a way that tries to right all of the wrongs of the past. Parenting to remedy our past won't fix what happened to us as children. We need to parent based on what is right and not what our parents got wrong.

5. ARE YOU PARENTING TO FIND YOUR WORTH?

A few years ago, we went away for a weekend vacation with my parents to Mackinac Island, Michigan. As we were heading back off the island one day, we had to squeeze on a nearly full boat. My parents, along with our kids, made their way to the front. Unfortunately we ran out of seats for all of us to sit together, so I found a seat a few rows away. We hadn't been on the water more than five minutes when my kids broke out a few snacks. And much to my surprise, the two older women behind me began to comment on what my children were eating.

"I can't believe those kids are eating potato chips," one said to another.

"They look too young to be eating chips. And on a boat?"

With each passing comment, I found myself struggling to think Jesus thoughts! Seriously! I couldn't even believe what I was hearing. I was growing angrier and angrier at their assessment of not only my children but also, by implication, my parenting. Little did they know those kids' mom was sitting right smack dab in front of them listening to their entire conversation (with smoke billowing from my ears). As I continued to listen to their ridicule, a heavy blanket of shame descended on me, even though I adamantly disagreed with them.

I'm still not sure why I let their comments upset me so much. But I can't help but be reminded that our children's behavior, whether for the good or the bad, can work its way into how worthy or worthless we feel as moms. When our kids are doing well, we feel worthy. When they are not, the weight of unworthiness settles in.

We need to be careful that we don't fall into letting our parenting define our worth. It is the gospel, the good news of Jesus, that ultimately steers us through the choppy waters of motherhood. Don't look to your mothering to find your worth; look to Jesus.

Every single one of us has parented in the wrong way. We have all at one time or another (and still do) let our desires, comparison, fear, or regrets rule in our parenting. In grace, God enables us to change our approach. God is the only perfect parent, and we can walk in freedom as we forge ahead in learning better ways.

Hard to Figure Out

A few years ago I was visiting a friend and mentor of mine. We were having a lovely time just chatting when she asked me, "So, which one of your children are you having trouble figuring out?"

I was a bit caught off guard when she asked me this question. But I was glad she'd asked. My husband and I had been at our wit's ends trying to figure out what would make a difference with one of our children. It wasn't that she was terribly rebellious or doing anything harmful, but there was definitely a disconnect with what we would say and how this child of ours would respond.

We had tried about everything.

Timeouts.

Lectures.

Consequences.

Nothing seemed to be registering, at least for lasting change.

"Tell me about her," my friend continued.

I shared with her a little about my child's personality and what she liked and disliked. I shared our history and some of the stories that would help her understand our parent-child relationship a little better.

My friend looked at me and said, "Well, she just needs to know you empathize with her."

"Empathize with her?" I said.

"Yes. She needs to know you hear her, understand her, and feel what she feels before you teach her."

I sat there for a moment, not knowing what to say at this uncomplicated answer to what I had been trying to figure out for months. This was a lightbulb moment for me.

"You mean everyone isn't just like me?" Hello, Ruth! I had been so focused on how *I* felt that I never even stopped to consider our differences and how my *child* was feeling.

I know it seems so simple. But for me it was a tremendous discovery. Up until this time I had never taken into consideration that my children were not like me. Their personalities are all different, and they look at life situations differently than I do. Everyday life looks different through their eyes than it looks through mine.

For instance, I am more of thinker than a feeler. If my child is a feeler, then my straightforward responses to her may seem harsh and indifferent. I can't understand why something is a big deal to her when it hardly makes a difference to me. We view a situation in two different ways, and instead of faulting my child for that, I need to understand her in order to reach her. I need to come alongside her and sympathize with her in that situation.

Now I'll admit it — it's not easy. Not one bit. It takes every ounce of my being not to burst out laughing at a situation that I find rather humorous, yet that she finds tragic. Or feel sympathetic when a situation looks more black and white to me. She is much more of a "feeler" than I. Now, of course there has to be a balance, and you have to help your child learn how to handle her personality in light of how God wants us to live, but you can't help her do that if you aren't viewing life through her lens. You won't be able to understand where she is coming from to help her in her journey of growth.

Right now as I sit here at my desk writing, my eye catches a large framed picture. On the picture matting all around the photo are the written words, "I love you, Mom. You're the best mom ever. Best friends. Bella + Mom = Best Friends." The framed picture is from my oldest daughter. The child I "just couldn't figure out."

I am so thankful that my friend spoke that truth into my life a few years ago. Her wise words changed the way I parented my daughter and helped me embrace our relationship. I had to intentionally (and still do) work hard at understanding her. But it has been so incredible to watch God knit our hearts together. I wouldn't trade all that hard work for anything.

In Search of a Better, Not Perfect, Way

As we talked about already, there are quite a few ways we can parent the wrong way. We can parent out of our own desires, out of fear, out of comparison, to remedy our past, or to find our own worth. All of us can get off track. We know there is no perfect method and no perfect path, but there are biblical guidelines that can help point us, and keep us, moving in the right direction. Let me summarize a few.

1. ACKNOWLEDGE DIFFERENCES AS STRENGTHS AND NOT WEAKNESSES.

God did not create humanity as generic human beings. He created them distinct by design. Each would be sculpted and shaped for different purposes.

It is amazing to me at what a young age these differences started to emerge in our children. We have two boys and two girls. While they share great similarities in some areas, they are drastically different in others.

Differences are good. They are part of God's design. But differences can cause confusion for parents. We have to be so careful that we don't treat our children as if they are identical. When we treat our children as identical we minimize their uniqueness. Be careful of viewing differences as deficiencies.

Differences can be expressed in a variety of ways. For example, there are significant differences between personalities. Some children are strong-willed, while others are gentle, sensitive to the slightest correction. Some children are more outgoing, talkative, and personable. Others are quieter, more reserved, thinking cautiously and calculating everything. These differences are not weaknesses.

I have two children who are quieter and two children who are more, how shall I say it … expressive. I tend to be a bit more like the second two, so I had to learn how to really step back, listen, and be aware of my quieter children so that I wouldn't squelch their unique personalities.

Another significant difference is in gender. In *Boys Adrift*, Dr. Leonard Sax explores the differences between boys and girls as it relates to education, discipline, performance, and more. In this incredibly helpful book we are reminded that gender really does play a role in how our children interact and function. For example, boys tend to be motivated by competition, while girls are more relationship- or friendship-oriented. Also, girls' brains develop a bit sooner, so girls are generally ready to learn to read and write sooner than most boys.[7] These are just a few simple examples, but I think being aware and educated on some of the differences between boys and girls can help us better understand our children and how to respond to them.

The goal of recognizing differences is to help our children grow into the unique people God intended for them to be. We need to help them discover that their gifts, personalities, and interests are all a part of his plan and his story.

2. PARENT AT A PACE THAT IS CONSISTENT WITH WHO YOUR CHILD IS.

Our culture has become highly competitive. It is really scary to see how many parents are driven by the fear of their child not measuring up. Kids are competing in sports and academics at a younger age and being pushed farther than they ever have before. The pressure is intense. Parents can be fearful that their kids are not going to be as prepared, cultured, or equipped to succeed. As a result, we not only pack our own schedules, but we also push our kids to the limits. In all of this frenzy, we throw aside and become blind to our child's uniqueness.

Uniqueness isn't just about who they will become; it is also about at what pace they will become that man or woman someday. No child's timing is the same. Trust me, I know it isn't easy to step off the fast track. But we have to be careful not to let the "markers" of our culture, a friend, or well-intentioned family members set the pace for our parenting.

Several years ago, George Barna published a book called *Revolutionary Parenting*. Full of research and helpful insight, he notes that parents naturally have a tendency to "hurry the development of their offspring." He writes,

> In our studies of what takes place in school classrooms and even Sunday school classes around the nation, we often have encountered the alarming trend of identifying what children "should" be like at a given age, along with the institutional push to make sure they reach that stage at the appointed time. In countless cases it has seemed as if children's development is being rushed to satisfy some ambiguous goal, robbing them of the delights of childhood in an effort to usher them into the responsibilities of adulthood prematurely ... sometimes we inadvertently "fast-track" personal development, eliminating the joy of growing at the pace God ordained for the person.[8]

It's so important for us to let our children run their race at *their* pace. The Christian life is often described as a race, so let's look at what the Bible says about how to run that race:

> Therefore, since we are surrounded by such a great cloud of witnesses, let us throw off everything that hinders and the sin that so easily entangles. And let us run with perseverance the race marked out for us, fixing our eyes on Jesus, the pioneer and perfecter of our faith.
>
> (HEBREWS 12:1–2)

This passage shows us that the Christian life isn't about how fast you run or even who comes in first. What matters is that you are putting one foot in front of the other and running toward the finish line. The writer encourages us to run *"the race marked out for us."* That phrase is critical to understand and has application for parenting the right way.

What is significant about that phrase? God doesn't call me to run someone else's race. He hasn't called me to compete in another family's race. He has called me to run the race that he has marked out for *me*. This is what can be so dangerous about comparing and competing. It ignores that God has created each child to be unique, including the pace at which our sons or daughters emerge into adulthood. Part of recognizing our child's uniqueness is understanding that they are developing at a pace that is specific to them.

So friend, run your race. Let your kids run their race. Don't be tempted to look over your shoulder at another person's course. Run yours, and let your kids run theirs!

3. Be a "generalist" and a "specialist."

This last application is about balancing the difference between being a "generalist" and a "specialist." Because our children are unique, this requires us to apply the truth of God's Word in different ways depending on the child. Let me explain the difference between these two terms.

The "generalist" understands that God has given us biblical principles that apply to all children and families. These commands are God's "general" instruction for us. So for example, God calls all parents to do the following:

- ❀ Raise their children to know and love God (Deuteronomy 6:4–9)
- ❀ Sacrificially love, nurture, protect, and provide for their children (1 Thessalonians 2:8, 11–12)
- ❀ Instruct children to respect authority (Ephesians 6:1–4)

  ❀ Establish biblical boundaries and appropriate disciplinary
consequences (Hebrews 12:7–11)

We could certainly add more instructions to this list. The point is
that God's Word does give us specific instruction on how to parent
the right way. Parenting is not a free-for-all or a "just hope for the
best" adventure! God gives these general instructions for all parents.
We understand that God has called all parents to shepherd and
teach God's Word. The family has been uniquely called to pass on
faith to the next generation.

But how we apply these principles may differ depending on our
children's gender, personality, and even age. This is the "specialist"
part of parenting. It requires that we wisely know our children,
understand their hearts, and know how to rightly apply the truth of
God's Word.

To be a "specialist" means I don't treat my children as if they are all
the same. For example, how we discipline our oldest daughter is
very different from how we discipline our youngest son. When she
was younger, she was more strong-willed, while our youngest son
was very sensitive. We would have done a great disservice to his
heart if we had treated him, and disciplined him, the same way we
did our daughter. To be a "specialist" requires really knowing your
child's heart and trusting God's Spirit to lead you.

Oh, friend, this is such an important point to understand. I
have seen all too many a child whose spirit was broken by an
overbearing parent or who was wild because of an overly permissive parent. Every child is different, and our parenting will look different for each child. I have been guilty too many times of forgetting
this critical reality.

4. PARENT WITH THE BIG PICTURE IN MIND.

Let's be honest — it is easy to get discouraged as a mom. You don't
have to be a mom for too long to feel worn out and weary. I'm not
just talking about being sleep deprived and physically wiped out.

Discouragement can creep in when you feel like you are failing. We grow weary when we sense we aren't getting through to our kids. We feel like we are disciplining for the same misbehavior over and over again. We fear they are never going to learn that lesson, correct that attitude, or change their mind. As moms, we can feel like we are losing battle after battle sometimes.

When we feel worn out, we need to remember the words of the apostle Paul: "Let us not become weary in doing good, for at the proper time we will reap a harvest if we do not give up" (Galatians 6:9).

This verse makes me want to weep almost every time I read it. I'm tired, and I am guessing you are too. "Let us not become weary," Paul writes, of "doing good." The command for us as moms is to keep "doing good," to keep faithfully shepherding our children in a way that honors God and his Word. Sometimes we don't see the fruit of our labor right away. And sometimes weariness may overtake us. In this we must avoid discouragement and focus instead on the harvest ahead.

There are going to be seasons, circumstances, or experiences that tempt us to be discouraged. But let's not lose sight of the big picture. Let's not take our eyes off Jesus. Sometimes in the "right now" we may feel like things aren't going to turn out well, but at "the proper time" we will receive a harvest if we do not give up. As moms, we need to have the perspective that this parenting gig is for the long haul. We can't judge the results or declare a final verdict too soon. We don't have to worry about doing it all right, because even when we get it wrong, and even when our children do wrong, our gracious Father is in control.

Don't give up, mom. Think of the harvest.

CHAPTER 11

Myth # 10:
My Child's Bad Choice
Means I'm a Bad Mom

Good parenting doesn't provide any surety your
kids will make good choices. That's true when your
toddler throws a fit at the zoo, and it's also true
when your son becomes a father at age sixteen.
You're not a failure if either of those things happen,
and neither is your child.

—Jill Savage and Dr. Kathy Koch,
No More Perfect Kids

It was a frosty February afternoon. The sun was trying its best to
peek its sunny smile out from behind the gray Midwestern clouds,
but those stubborn puffs of glum simply refused to move along and
drag the gloomy winter atmosphere with them. I (Karen) sat cross-
legged on my living room floor, robotically folding laundry while
catching up on the world's happenings by watching a television
news update.

As I folded and listened, something caught my eye. My fifteen-year-
old son's permission slip for a school function sat folded on the

kitchen island. It had been placed there as a reminder for him to tote it to school since it was due that day.

Now, this child happens to be rather forgetful. So, I did my best each day to help to jog his memory without rescuing him or enabling him to continue his scatterbrained ways. In fact, we'd enacted a parental policy with this often-forgetful son. It was the "three strikes and you're out" rule. If he forgot a textbook, permission slip, or money, I would run it up to him at the school, but only three times. After that he was out of luck. And with each of those three times, it would be a five-dollar charge. (Hey, it was a way to pay for my lattes.)

Well, this was February—two-thirds of the way through the school year—and it was only his first strike. (He was making progress!) So I decided to take the forgotten paper to the high school, about a five-minute drive from home. It was due by his next class period so there was no time to run a comb through my unwashed hair or spruce up my face with a little makeup. I'd just bop into the office for a second, drop off the form, and get back to my ordinary day as a mom.

When I entered the office, the secretary greeted me, and she asked me to take a seat. I found it strange for someone just dropping off a permission slip, and so I began to question her. But before I could let my question escape my lips, she said, "The assistant principal will be with you shortly."

Puzzled as to why he needed to speak with me, I started to ask what he needed to see me about. It was then that I noticed that there was a student sitting in the line of chairs along the far office wall. That student was my son. And he looked awful. The color had completely drained from his face, leaving his skin looking as pale and gray as the mid-Michigan winter sky.

Assuming he had fallen ill and needed to go home, I started to speak to him. But he beat me to it, starting a conversation first. Without looking up from the ground, he quietly whispered, "You and Dad are going to be so mad."

Just then, the vice principal's office door slowly creaked open. "I will see you now, Mrs. Ehman," he declared. I was totally unprepared for what he was about to tell me.

I hesitantly walked in and lowered myself into the padded chair across from the vice principal's desk. I felt like I was marching into court, although unsure what the charge against me was. He wasted no time in telling me about the situation that had transpired that day that included my son.

One of my son's friends was confronted in class for a bottle of peach iced tea that he had with him on his desk. It wasn't against the rules to have something to drink in the classroom. The problem was that the teacher suspected it was not full of tea but rather of tobacco juice from chewing tobacco. Upon further investigation she discovered that this was true.

That student was marched down to the office and promptly suspended from school. Being in possession of a tobacco product in our state is unlawful if you are under the age of eighteen. Beyond that, students at the high school—whether they are eighteen or not—are forbidden from having any tobacco products on the school premises. When the student was questioned as to where he got that tobacco, he 'fessed up. He told the school official he had gotten it from my son.

My son was then called down to the office. The investigation continued. It was not only true that he had supplied his underage friend with the chewing tobacco, he also had a couple more tins in his backpack he was going to deliver to other boys in the ninth grade!

My baby boy was helping to run an illegal tobacco ring!

It seems a strong-personality, bully-type senior boy—who *was* of legal age to purchase tobacco products—was buying tins for underage freshman. A savvy-enough criminal to know that getting caught on school property with the stuff meant expulsion, he'd hoodwinked my happy-go-lucky, leap-before-you-look, naïve child into being the go-between, delivering the contraband stuff to the underclassmen. For his efforts, my child was being given a kickback of cash.

That little business arrangement now cost my son a six-day suspension from school. But that wasn't all. "Well, Mrs. Ehman," the administrator continued, "I actually should call the police since your son is a minor in possession of a tobacco product, which is illegal."

A crack opened in the tense conversation. It seemed he was inviting me to plead for my son, to make the case that he'd never been in trouble at the school before. That he was an athlete. He'd been on the student council. He was a good kid who made a bad choice. I felt an invitation to plead for mercy for my son so this would not go on his permanent record.

I shot a quick prayer toward the sterile white ceiling. Then I opened my mouth. I couldn't believe the words that came out.

"You could call the police?"

He nodded.

"Then, sir, please do."

He picked up the phone and began to dial. With each punch of his finger and beep of the phone, my mind ticked off the bad decisions this boy had made, decisions that also made me look bad, now shrinking in disgrace.

A police officer was summoned. The ten minutes it took to arrive seemed like an eternity. I tried to make small talk while we waited—the professional school administrator in his fancy suitcoat and the humiliated mom wearing her sweatpants and her shame.

When the policeman entered the room, my heart again sank. I knew this officer. I'd known him for over a quarter century. He had been a high school student in our youth group when my husband was a youth pastor two decades earlier. Of all the officers that could have been dispatched, it had to be him!

Together this team of three unlikely cohorts strategized about what was best for this serious situation at hand. I did not plead for leniency. In fact, my exact words to the officer were, "Please don't just give him a slap on the wrist. I'd like you to find the biggest book you can, and I will help you chuck it at him!"

In the end, my child was issued a tobacco ticket and summoned to appear in court for breaking the law. What transpired in the following weeks was a court appearance, a fine, assigned community service hours, and a sealed record as a juvenile offender! The court referee, whom my son and I both appeared before, had mercy on him. He ordered him to serve his community service hours, but told him that he could get out of the $100 fine if he wrote a report on the dangers and pitfalls of tobacco products.

This incident brought about two of my lowest days as a mom. You see, not only did he do wrong and get busted, but it all went down in a very public way and in front of people whom I'd known for years.

Yes, I knew the police officer. But I also knew the school administrative assistant that had been sitting in the office the day I'd arrived. She and her family attended the church where my husband had been a youth pastor years before. That was bad day number one. Then came bad day number two. The juvenile court referee? That was not his only job as a referee. He was also a basketball ref for our local homeschool league and had officiated many games for both of my boys for several years when they were homeschooled. He'd also worked on community projects with my husband during his youth pastor days. We knew him well, and he knew our passion for raising godly youth who would make a difference in the community.

Oh, please.

With each encounter with these folks, my face grew redder, my heart knew more pain, my soul felt increased shame. I tethered my child's wrong choice to the core of my identity and then decided I was a failure as a mom. A complete and utter failure. A former pastor's wife turned Bible teacher and author who somehow couldn't teach her own son to obey the law—or the Lord.

Multiple-Choice Mothering

As my three children have gotten older—two now adults and one in his last year of high school—I am seeing how very much I as a mom latched on to our final myth of motherhood: My child's bad choice means I'm a bad mom.

From the moment our child emerges from the womb, or we pick her up for adoption at the appointed adoption location, we get a front-row seat in watching our child behave. At times their behavior makes our hearts sing. Their first smiles. First steps. Watching their darling personalities emerge. Some things they do might invoke laughter, or a bout with serious sickness may bring out the most sympathetic feelings we have in our mama hearts. Each day that passes finds us falling more and more in love with them.

However, there are some detours along the way. Our child may do or say something that causes us alarm. Even embarrassment or anger. Or maybe she just threatens to make us look like we don't really know what in the world we are doing in parenting a child because her behavior is exasperating, not exemplary.

I remember bringing our first child home from the hospital when she was four days old. Although it had been a long labor that ended in an emergency C-section, I simply adored being known as a mom. I had studied hard. Observed others. I felt ready to take on the enormous task and responsibility of raising my auburn-haired, hazel-eyed bundle of joy, even though there were still things I was unsure of. I just knew that with enough hard work and diligent effort, I could figure it all out. I would apply all of the knowledge from the books I read and from the other mothers who seemed to be pros. All would go well.

Then came the first day we took our new baby to church. Instead of sweetly sleeping through the sermon, she began to cry. And boy, did that girl have a set of lungs on her! (Still does.)

Now I had this nifty little equation cemented in my mind. It went like this: crying baby = bad mom. Oh, and this wasn't the only equation I had tucked inside my intellect. There were also other things that equaled a bad mom. A toddler throwing a tantrum. A bully on the kindergarten playground who pushed another child down. A preteen with an attitude who rolled her eyes at an adult and flippantly said "What-evvvver" when being asked to do something. A teen that broke the rules. Or broke the law. All of these things I felt could be traced directly back to the child having a bad mom.

Well, at least one of my children has done all of the above! I guess that puts me in bold contention for worst mom of the year. Or decade.

Oh, my.

Or does it?

Bad Boys (and Girls) of the Bible

Through the ages parents have felt responsible for and bemoaned their kid's behavior. In fact, the Bible records stories of many children whose behavior was enough to give their parents premature gray hair.

Consider, for instance, the Old Testament character Job. In the very first chapter of the book that bears his name we spy him getting up early to offer burnt offerings for each of his ten children—seven boys and three girls—after they had been at a ruckus-raising party the evening before. Take a peek at this parent's morning routine: "When a period of feasting had run its course, Job would make arrangements for them to be purified. Early in the morning he would sacrifice a burnt offering for each of them, thinking, 'Perhaps my children have sinned and cursed God in their hearts.' This was Job's regular custom" (Job 1:5).

Job worried that his darling dependents may have messed up. Behaved badly. Even sinned. And so he did what he could to make sure these blots were lifted from their record. And he did this over and over and over again each morning even before he had poured his first cup of joe.

Job's desire to have his kids walk in a worthy manner is admirable. We *should* be concerned for our children's spiritual state. Concerned about, but not totally responsible for. And do you catch something in the story here? You might not if the person of Job is new to you. (Oh, by the way, his name is pronounced with a long "o." Rhymes with "robe." Yes, "Job wore a robe" is how I remembered it as a girl.)

Wait ... where was I?

Oh yes, while his kids may have been rabble-rousers, Job was not. In fact, Scripture records that "there is no one on earth like him; he is blameless and upright, a man who fears God and shuns evil" (Job 1:8). And it wasn't just some local ancient reporter making this observation. That description was uttered by the Lord himself!

Impeccable parent. Iffy kids. It happens.

How about another example? Do you remember the story of Eli's sons? The story is found in 1 Samuel chapters 1 and 2, should you want to read it for yourself, but here is the *Reader's Digest* condensed version:

Eli was a kindhearted and upright priest who ministered to Hannah when she was in a tight spot. Hannah was infertile and would pray to the Lord at the temple, weeping and asking him for a child. Eli heard her and, after investigating to make sure she wasn't drunk, he delivered the news to her that she would have a son. She responded by saying she would give the son to the Lord. So once the child was weaned, Eli raised her son Samuel, providing a home for him as well as spiritual training. But Samuel was not the only person for whom

Eli was a father figure. He also had two sons of his very own flesh and blood. Their names were Hophni and Phinehas. Part of the duties of Eli's offspring was to serve as priests in the tabernacle at Shiloh. It was here that the Ark of the Covenant was kept.

Their job description included functioning as mediators between God and the people as they worshiped and offered sacrifices. You would think, with having such a profound religious responsibility, that these two boys would be the cream of the crop spiritually. Not so. Instead, these two brothers "did not know the LORD" (1 Samuel 2:12 ESV). They also were referred to as the sons of Belial (KJV). Belial means "wicked" or "worthless," and that was exactly what these brothers were.

They were greedy. And lustful. They were extortionists, taking from the people the best meat that was brought in for sacrifices and using it for themselves. Instead of properly boiling the meat and eating only what the Law allowed, they instead insisted on the best cuts to roast. These had not had the fat burned away, as was required by the Law. Thus they treated the Lord's offerings with contempt.

But wait! There's more. They not only abused authority, they also committed immoral acts with women who had come to the tabernacle.

Their father Eli found out about all of their behavior. And so he had a little meeting with his sons to ask why in the world they were committing such sins:

> Now Eli, who was very old, heard about everything his sons were doing to all Israel and how they slept with the women who served at the entrance to the tent of meeting. So he said to them, "Why do you do such things? I hear from all the people about these wicked deeds of yours. No, my sons; the report I hear spreading among the LORD's people is not good. If one person sins against another, God may mediate for the offender; but if anyone sins against the LORD, who will intercede for them?" His sons, however, did not listen to their father's rebuke, for it was the LORD's will to put them to death.

(1 SAMUEL 2:22–25)

So to boil this all down (no pun intended), an awesome man had awful sons. He tried to correct them, but they would not listen. As a result the Lord dealt harshly with them.

The Bible does record that Eli was warned to remove them from their duties, but he simply couldn't bring himself to do so. His sons then died on the same day, and Eli's surrogate son, Samuel, went on to become the new prophet for Israel.

While Eli was not a perfect parent—as none of us are—he was not called wicked as his sons were. He could have made the decision to remove his misbehaving sons from their priestly duties, preventing further corruption, but it is never recorded that their bad behavior was his fault in the first place.

The lesson learned? If our children are behaving badly, we must do what we can to confront them about their behavior, urging them to stop. This Eli did. What he failed to do was follow through with some consequences for their actions.

You see, we can do every Bible study released, highlighting and underlining and memorizing each suggested passage. We can keep away from evil practices ourselves, dealing speedily with our own sin. However, sometimes we just can't bring ourselves to deal swiftly with the sin of our child.

It is possible to be a godly *person* but fail to be a godly *parent*.

Let this serve as a warning that we need to be proactive and timely to deliver consequences if our kids don't alter their behavior based on just a verbal warning from us. But we also should be aware of the fact that two bad apples fell from a tree (Eli) that looked pretty good. If we have children behaving wickedly, it is not our fault. They must answer for their own sins. It is our responsibility, however, to try to help them to correct their behavior and change the path they are on. And we must be ready to follow through with uncomfortable and unpopular punishment if it is needed.

Another family in the Bible has always fascinated me when it comes to trying to pin the bad behavior of a child on the shoulders of a parent. Think of the story of Cain and Abel. They were the sons in the very first family. Their parents were Adam and Eve.

Cain was the very first man born into the world. His brother Abel was the very first one to die. And how did he die? At the hands of his brother.

Cain, we are told in the book of Genesis, was a man who tended to the crops. His kid brother was a sheepherder. A little jealous drama ensued between the brothers over the fact that the Lord accepted Abel's offering of some of the firstborn of his flock along with portions of their fat. Cain had brought some produce as an offering, but it didn't draw the same favored reaction from God. As a result, it greatly ticked off Cain. So one day he lured his unsuspecting brother out into the field and promptly terminated him.

Two sons. Different likes and passions. Different personalities. Extremely different character qualities. One was innocent. One committed murder. Both had the same parents. Were their parents responsible for their actions and choices?

If you can draw the conclusion that how a child turns out is directly the parents' sole responsibility, then how do you account for these two mismatched brothers? Wouldn't they both have turned out exemplary or both emerged as horrid? How did one grow to be a mind-your-own-business, likeable sort, and the other grow up to be the first one to have his mug shot nailed up to the local post office wall? Were Adam and Eve responsible for these boys' actions?

No. Their choices were their own.

Hundreds of pages later, in Luke 15, we also see two brothers who be-have very differently. The story of the prodigal son showcases an older son who doesn't outwardly cause any trouble. He goes with the flow. Keeps to the program. A model child, or so it seems.

His younger brother, however, decides to wander off to a far land and squander his portion of his father's inheritance on women and a wild lifestyle. Later however, while hungry and envying the food he feeds to the pigs in his job as a swine keeper, he comes to his senses. He returns home to his father, who welcomes him with open arms.

It is then that the seemingly virtuous brother shows some villainy in his character. Jealous of his dad's affection for the black sheep of the family, he refuses to attend the party thrown for his formerly wayward brother. In fact, he points out that no one ever held a big goat roast for *him* the entire time he was home behaving and being the good son.

Both of these boys had character flaws, even though their father is depicted as loving and a good provider. Again, their choices were made of their own volition. Their bad behavior was not the fault of their dad.

So what can we learn from this little trip through the Bible, perusing parents and their progeny? A few things. First...

1. It is a parent's duty to teach their children about the Lord and what he requires.

There are scads of verses in the Bible that instruct parents to instruct their kids. We see early in the Bible, as the Lord was instructing the Israelites how to live in the way that he requires, that they were to be certain to pass along all the info to the kiddos too. And they were to be intentional in talking to their sons and daughters about all the good things God does in their lives. Deuteronomy 4:9 shows this concept: "Only be careful, and watch yourselves closely so that you do not forget the things your eyes have seen or let them fade from your heart as long as you live. Teach them to your children and to their children after them."

A few chapters later, we see the classroom we should use to transfer these truths to our children. It is the classroom of life:

Fix these words of mine in your hearts and minds; tie them as symbols on your hands and bind them on your foreheads. Teach them to your children, talking about them when you sit at home and when you walk along the road, when you lie down and when you get up. Write them on the doorframes of your houses and on your gates, so that your days and the days of your children may be many in the land the LORD swore to give your ancestors, as many as the days that the heavens are above the earth.

(DEUTERONOMY 11:18–21)

So today we might think of it this way: Talk about God's laws and what he has done in your life when you eat a formal dinner or just sit and snack in the living room. When you are driving in the car or waiting in line in the carpool. Text biblical encouragement to them when they are away with their friends. Work a verse into your conversation as you are tucking them in at night. Hang Scripture signs in your home. Anything you can do to get the Word of God in front of their eyes, wafting into their ears, and solidified in their hearts. Our kids need to know what is required of them by God so they can learn to make decisions according to his ways.

2. IT IS A PARENT'S DUTY TO MODEL FOR THEIR CHILDREN A GROWING RELATIONSHIP WITH JESUS AND WHAT HE PROVIDES.

Just knowing what God requires of us isn't enough. Our kids must know where (or better yet to whom) to go to be empowered to live the Christian life. Don't be a private Christ-follower, never allowing your kids to see your relationship with him up close. Of course we don't want to practice good deeds in front of our kids simply to be noticed. However, we should allow them to get a glimpse of what a real walk with Christ looks like.

Talk with them about your relationship with God. What are you learning as you read your Bible today? Is there a particular lesson that has really hit home for you in your Bible study group or small group at church? Don't just share the concepts with your close friends; talk out loud about them with your children. Of course, if your children are very small, you may have to break it down for them, telling them only the very basics of the biblical truth and giving it to them on a level they can understand. Seeing you excited about what the Bible says and how it is coming to life for you can be contagious. Your children can be infected early with the Bible bug!

Also let them see that prayer works. Tell them what you are praying about currently. Give them specific requests for them to pray about too. As God answers, discuss his answers with your children. It is helpful to teach them from early on that God is not some genie in a bottle, where we rub our hands together in prayer and then stand back and watch him grant our every wish.

I have told my children often, when discussing how God answers prayer, that it is much in the way that their dad and I answer them. When they make a request, perhaps to have a friend spend the night, we can answer them one of three ways: yes, no, or not right now. This is much in the same way that God answers us. He knows what ultimately is best for us. Saying that he answers prayers does not mean that he always gives us the answer of yes to each and every little thing we desire.

Being an on-purpose parent means we let our children see us conversing with God, applying his Word, and completely trusting his wisdom and will.

3. If our children misbehave when they are small, it might be due in part to our lack of instruction.

Yes. There is truth to the statement that if a young child misbehaves in some situations, it might be due in part to the lack of training by a parent. Is four-year-old Junior helping himself to some candy-striped gum at the store, pocketing it without paying a penny? Well, if mom and dad never taught him that such behavior is against the law, then of course they helped to bring about the sticky situation of this Juicy Fruit juvenile. Misbehaving and out-of-control young children are sometimes due in part to lackadaisical parenting. A failure to teach children right from wrong or to impart proper behavior and manners can lead to bad behavior in a young child. However, the older the child gets, the more responsibility must be put on her shoulders.

When you have been diligent to teach your child right from wrong and they are a preteen or older, resist the urge to label yourself a bad mom if she makes a wrong choice.

4. IF OUR CHILDREN DO WRONG WHEN THEY ARE PRETEENS, TEENS, OR ADULTS, WE SHOULD HELP TO GUIDE THEM BACK TO THE RIGHT PATH WITHOUT BEATING OURSELVES UP FOR THE WRONG TURN THEY TOOK.

Oh, this is so hard! Our human nature wants to lash out, to holler and scream, "WHAT WERE YOU THINKING!?!?!" Chances are, they weren't. Teens, especially of the male sort, don't always think before they act. In fact, the decision-making part of their brain isn't fully developed until they are about twenty-five years old! We expect them to make decisions as we would—we who are adults, with experience and fully developed brains. But they don't always. We must help to correct them. Dish out consequences too. But we *must not* beat ourselves up over their bad choices.

And when our kids do make bad choices, we must still continue to be a parent—guiding them, loving them, and cheering them on. It doesn't mean we wink at their wrongdoing, passing it off as no big deal. It does mean we fight the urge to blow up and shame, condemn, and reject.

One of my friends found out her college-age daughter was pregnant out of wedlock, the result of a bad decision one night at a party with a guy she barely knew. As my friend wisely told me, "When you want them the least is when they need you the most."

My friend Cindy, who is a speaker and an author of Bible studies, texted me once, desperate for prayer for her child. I've asked her to share her story with you:

> I'll never forget when I received an early morning frantic phone call from my college-age son, "Um, Mom, I've got a situation." Through his weeping and blubbering, my son shared a series of very poor, devastating choices that ended up with police involvement and possibly very serious and life-changing legal charges.

At the moment of my son's call, my thoughts were focused on listening intently to what my son was revealing, while simultaneously praying God would infuse me with his divine wisdom and words. This was beyond dreadful, and I was desperate for God to guide us—step by step by step—through this difficult and complicated situation.

Later that evening, after the initial shock wore off, my mind began to process the implications of my son's choices. What if my son is arrested? How do I explain that to our three younger children? What would the neighbors think? What if this made our local newspaper? How would I go to the school functions, my speaking engagements, my MOPS talks—knowing my firstborn son was involved with not just poor choices, but illegal, damaging decisions.

My worst nightmare was coming true right before my very eyes, and I didn't know what to do.

Initially, my thoughts were focused on helping my son at the moment. I knew this was a life-changing situation (however it played out), and I desperately needed God to work through me. I did not want to respond in the flesh. Although on the inside I was wondering, "How could he have done this? Did I not raise him better? What in the world is going on here?"—thankfully I was able to demonstrate much unconditional love, grace, compassion, and empathy. This was clearly a work of the Lord.

Cindy was such an example of a mom who refused to go into panic mode and freak out. Although it was incredibly hard, I watched my friend pour out her heart to the Lord while she poured out compassion and love on her son. He already knew she did not approve of his actions. There was no need for a lecture. There was a need for unconditional love. And my faith was stretched too as I got daily texts updates of how I could pray. And, when it was over, I told her to tell that boy of hers he owed Miss Karen a new pair of jeans. Mine were worn clear through at the knees from praying for him!

I'm so thankful that we are not bad moms just because our child makes a bad choice. It is hard enough dealing with our own choices sometimes. Besides, think of it this way—if you are directly and solely responsible for your child's bad behavior, then is the flip side also true? Should you take credit for their good and godly choices? No. Anything good and godly in my kids finds all the credit going to God. They make right choices *despite* my being their parent, because I am imperfect. Any bad choices they make, they own.

5. SOMETIMES OUR CHILDREN'S BAD BEHAVIOR CONTINUES BECAUSE WE FAIL TO ISSUE CONSEQUENCES.

In loving our kids when they have done wrong, let's be careful not to repeat Eli's mistake and only warn our kids to stop without telling them what consequences will happen if they don't. When our kids are not following the laws of the land or of the Lord, let's not be afraid to confront them. We can be instrumental in helping them to get back on the right, and righteous, path.

6. DON'T RAISE A HERD.

While there is merit in having the same rules for all of your children when it comes to issues such as curfew, dating, and such, resist the urge to raise a herd. Children must be treated as individuals. The same discipline will not always work for every child. They have different personalities. They have different reactions to different consequences.

When our children were smaller, we realized that we needed to give out a different consequence to each child for misbehaving. One simply could not stand having to do extra work around the house such as mopping floors or pulling weeds. Her brother, however, loved hard work. If we made him pull the weeds in the herb garden, it wouldn't bother him at all. He would actually enjoy it. For this child we issued monetary consequences. He hated parting with his cash! The third child was not deterred by either of these consequences. But, boy oh boy, don't take away a social gathering from him—to this day! When he misbehaved as a young boy, he had to miss a birthday party or ice skating outing. That was what hurt him most.

Proverbs 22:6 states: "Train up a child in the way he should go; even when he is old he will not depart from it" (ESV).

The original language in the verse makes it read more like this, as translated in the Amplified Version of the Bible, "Train up a child in the way he should go [and in keeping with his individual gift or bent], and when he is old he will not depart from it."

Other biblical scholars say it literally means "according to their bent." This would indicate that we need to be students of our kids, to study how they are wired and then be very careful about how we interact with them, especially when it comes to discipline. So resist the urge to come up with uniform policies and perfunctory consequences. Ask God to give you creative consequences that will be effective. You might have to mix things up a bit for each individual child in order to get the most bang for your parenting buck.

Which leads us to the next point ...

7. RAISE YOUR CHILDREN ON YOUR KNEES.

Most crucial. Most needed. But sometimes, most overlooked. Especially if you are a "doer." Doers like to do. Moms who are doers think they should not just sit there but should do something. Sometimes prayer feels like just sitting there. But we have to get this notion out of our brains. Prayer is the most crucial thing when it comes to raising our children. We must raise our children on our knees. Going to God in times of crisis and in times of joy helps to solidify our relationship with him and helps to bring about change in the life of our children. So pray, mom, PRAY!

8. REMIND YOURSELF THAT EVERYTHING GOOD IN YOUR CHILD IS STILL THERE.

My friend Glynnis told me this once when I was lamenting to her on the telephone about the chewing tobacco incident. I thought this child was a hopeless cause because he had been duped into making a wrong choice. But my friend's words encouraged me. It helped me to remember all of the good things about my son. They were still there; I just couldn't see them because his bad choice eclipsed them and made me forget all of his wonderful qualities.

He is compassionate, always rooting for the underdog or wanting to help anyone he knows who is down on his luck. He is creative. And he has amazing social skills. In fact, once the incident had blown over, I saw that some of his good qualities actually were present in his bad decision. He saw an opportunity to be an entrepreneur by helping run that illegal tobacco ring. Of course his decision in that case was dead wrong, but a few years later when he took economics at school, we saw that he is a very gifted businessman with a keen sense of economics. In fact, at the age of seventeen he is already saving to start a Roth IRA and a 401(k) as soon as he is legally able.

Also, we discovered that the older boy who was purchasing tobacco came from a horrible family situation and had very little money. My son said he felt sorry for him and wanted to help him out. Again, this does not excuse the poor choice to participate in the shady deal, but it does reveal the compassionate heart of my son.

And remember the court referee told my son he wouldn't have to pay the fine if he wrote a paper about the health dangers of tobacco products? He wrote it and turned it in to the court. I thought the incident was all over and done with when one day I saw the court's phone number pop up on my caller ID. Afraid something was wrong, I hesitantly answered. It was the court official calling to tell me that my son's paper was so well-researched and written that they were now using it as an example in our county and sending copies to the neighboring county's juvenile court as well. He just wanted to let me know I should be proud of him. I sheepishly replied, "Well, sir, thank you … I think?"

So remember—even when your child makes a bad choice—everything good is still in him (or her)!

9. REMIND YOURSELF THAT YOU ARE SEEING THE BEGINNING OF THEIR TESTIMONY.

Once when I was especially distraught over a not-so-hot choice one of my kids had made, I called my friend Lynn. Through my sobs, she heard my heartache and told me exactly the words I needed to hear right then. "Karen, you have to remind yourself that you are seeing the beginning of their testimony. This is not the end."

Her words caused me to stop the runaway monologue in my head that was droning on and on about my child's bad behavior. Instead, I suddenly recalled all of the wonderful people I know today who have a wild testimony. Many of them are sold-out for Christ and serving him in amazing ways. But they all had made horrible choices as a teen or young adult. Some were immoral. Some were against the law. All were downright wrong. However, despite their bad choices early on in their lives, God drew them to himself and they responded. Their testimonies are powerful and show to others the compassion and forgiveness of a holy and mighty God.

Mom, God is greater than the fallout from the choices of your small child. He is greater than the bad decisions they might make during their elementary school years. He is far greater than the consequences of their wrong choices as a teen. And he is greater still than what heartache they may bring to you when they are adults.

Do not tether your identity to the choices of your child, whether stellar or stupid. We are not our child's choices. Their choices and their behavior are their own.

CHAPTER 12

No Longer Hoodwinked

It takes the eye of faith to see the fruit of a coming generation of faithfulness.

—NANCY WILSON

Her arms swung around me (Ruth), clutching my neck. Leaning in close, almost nose to nose, she declared, "You're the best mommy in the whole world!" My heart melted like it usually does when my sweet five-year-old makes such statements. What mom doesn't love to hear her child declare such love? I breathed a deep sigh and whispered, "Mom loves you sooooo much!" "Me love you too," she hoarsely whispered back.

I have these exchanges quite often with my children. But this particular time, I had something else going on inside of me as my daughter was so boldly declaring her devotion. I had a heaviness on my heart that she was completely unaware of. What she didn't know is that deep down I wasn't feeling like "the best mommy in the whole world." Instead, I felt like a mess. A big mess.

It had been a very stressful season in my life, and I wasn't the mom I had been for the last ten years. After suddenly losing my father-in-law to a tragic car accident and my mother-in-law just two years later, all in the midst of leaving the church my husband had been on staff at for ten years to move to a new church in a new town with new friends, I had let the overwhelming circumstances I found myself in crowd my mind and heart. A smile was harder to come by, and I felt the joy being sucked right out of my days. Magnifying my personal state, through all of this I had let the nagging voices of doubt fill my head, and I began to question whether I really was a good mom at all.

I was tired.

I was feeling worn out.

I was struggling to keep up and keep it all together.

Most days, as soon as I took the last sip of my morning coffee, I was longing for bedtime. I was fully aware that I needed to make a change. As I wrestled through how I felt, I kept coming back to the same conclusion over and over again. I knew I needed to make a change.

What I had to come to grips with was glaringly obvious.

That change needed to begin with *me*.

John 3:30 is my life verse. It has a humbling reminder for us all: "He must become greater; I must become less."

God has woven this verse through my life right from when I first became a Christian. As a teenager, I unfolded a small piece of paper that had been passed on from my youth pastor to a friend of mine who was in charge of being sure I got the note. Written on the paper were the words, "He must become greater; I must become less." I hadn't been a Christian long and hadn't been regularly attending youth group. To be honest, I had been somewhat avoiding church. This was the gentle reminder I needed to get back on track. It was a pivotal, life-changing moment for me.

All I needed was to read that simple verse and I knew that I was living for the wrong thing entirely. Myself. It was time to follow Jesus. Really follow him. I have had to stand firm and hold on steady to this verse, because it is a daily battle to relinquish my will to his. Time and time again I have needed to walk by faith and not by my feelings. As a mom some twenty years later, it is no different. Feeling the heaviness and guilt and believing the lie that I was a bad mom, I stood at the same crossroads with that same call to surrender. *"He must become greater; I must become less."*

Owning your life has to be a daily, step-by-step surrender to the One who orders and owns your steps. You see, we all have hard times in our lives, trying seasons that can last months, years, or even a lifetime. Not one of us is immune. But there is one thing that we can all do. We can choose how we will face the life we live each and every day. We can choose to own our life.

God has given each of us a unique story and purpose. He is writing a story through us. It is his story, but in grace, he transforms ours to be a part of his. As moms, a huge part of our stories are the lives that we pour into every single day at home.

Will you live that story?

Will you own it and glorify God through it?

What kind of legacy will you leave?

Living a Legacy

One of my favorite passages of Scripture relating to legacy is Hebrews 11, a chapter that some Bible teachers call the "Hall of Faith" because it records the legacy of men and women who walked by faith.

There is a constant refrain throughout the chapter: "By faith ..." For example, look at this snippet:

> By faith Isaac blessed Jacob and Esau in regard to their future.
>
> By faith Jacob, when he was dying, blessed each of Joseph's sons, and worshiped as he leaned on the top of his staff.

> By faith Joseph, when his end was near, spoke about the exodus
> of the Israelites from Egypt and gave instructions concerning the
> burial of his bones.
>
> By faith Moses' parents hid him for three months after he was
> born, because they saw he was no ordinary child, and they were
> not afraid of the king's edict.
>
> (HEBREWS 11:20–23)

Do you see those two beautiful words in of each of these stories? It was *by faith* they left their mark. It was by faith they lived their life. It was by faith that their legacy still echoes today.

You'll notice, especially if you know the Bible well, that the names mentioned here and elsewhere in the chapter were not the names of perfect people. They were not saints in the sense that they were without sin. They were far from even holy at times. But they were available. They had hearts that were wide open to God's love. Their lives were wrapped around that all-consuming desire to do whatever they did for God.

And I think what is most amazing about the men and women in this chapter is that their legacy was largely unknown to them. I can't help but wonder what each of them would think if they read their names in this "Hall of Faith." Would the fruit of their obedience take them by surprise? Would they be shocked at what followed in the wake of their lives?

These were men and women simply trying to be obedient to God. They wanted more than anything to please him, the One to whom they owed everything. Their story was caught up in the amazing story of God. Sometimes faith is more about putting one foot in front of the other than it is living with the hair on the back of your neck standing straight up. Sometimes the big stuff, the stuff that echoes for eternity, is all wrapped up in the little stuff. It's found in the trenches: in the middle of dirty diapers, story times, meals, and car rides.

Whatever you do, and wherever you are, do it for God. Let your life leave a legacy for God's glory. Allow God to write your own chapter as a part of his much greater story.

"By faith …"

By faith Kelly loved and nurtured her baby, building an intimate bond that would help her child eventually understand and experience the love of her Father God.

By faith Allison disciplined her children, teaching them to understand right from wrong.

By faith Emily enrolled her child in piano lessons, where he thrived, and quietly she thanked God for her child's unique gifts and interests.

By faith, over many years, Janice faithfully set aside money so her children could attend a Christian college, where their understanding of faith and the world would be shaped by fellow believers.

By faith Anna prayed daily for her children, entrusting them to the care of their heavenly Father.

By faith …

Time to Live the Truth

Just as Ruth believed a myth about herself the day her sweet daughter gave her such encouraging words, we moms are often tempted to believe the lies floating around in our minds, threatening to knock the confidence out of our mothering. Ruth and I (Karen) pray that over the course of experiencing this book with us, you have begun to recognize some of these fables and replace them with the truth. God's truth.

Let's revisit them one last time to make sure we stop dwelling in the land of motherhood mythology. You see, when we start to believe the myths—and then live in defeat because of what they tempt us to believe—we never quite measure up. And then? Then we apologize. We apologize for what failures we are. We apologize for not living up to others' expectations of us. Or perhaps, just in our minds, we beat ourselves up over and over again for not being able to be all that culture says we should be—all those things we think other mothers are being when we spy their perfect profiles on social media.

So let's stop the mythology. Let's stop the apology. Don't believe the lies! Don't apologize. Hold your head high, mom. You and God have got this!

(Okay. End of pep talk. Putting the pom-poms down now.)

One more time, let's go over the ten myths moms believe. And let's kick them to the curb forever!

MYTH #1: MOTHERING IS NATURAL, EASY, AND INSTINCTIVE

While most women feel the natural *desire* to be a mom, that doesn't necessarily mean we have the natural *ability* to be a mom. Like everything in life, motherhood takes time, intentional effort, and lifelong learning. Just as you didn't automatically know how to cook, drive a car, or excel in the marketplace, you don't automatically know all that is involved in being a good mom. We all have to learn.

Embarking on the journey of motherhood is an experience none of us can be fully prepared for. No matter how many times we told ourselves that mothering would be easy, it just isn't. As a little girl, I dreamed of being a mom someday. Whether that is your story or not, my dream didn't match up at all with the reality of motherhood. The truth behind the myth is that wanting to be a mom and knowing how to be a mom are two different things!

MYTH #2: THE WAY I MOTHER IS THE RIGHT (AND ONLY) WAY

No. No, sweetheart, it isn't. Neither is the way I'm doing it. And no one is doing it exactly "right." Unless there is a black-and-white commandment in Scripture for something that pertains to our mothering, raising your kiddos is multiple choice. Are some choices better than others? Of course they are! We shouldn't just cast lots, or close our eyes and spin around and then pin our hopes and dreams on some random method of parenting. We should be prayerful. And careful. We should weigh opinions of other trusted mentors and mothers who are further down the road than we are. But we must stop short of thinking we are doing things the right and only way.

And so what if there was a right way to carry out an aspect of mothering? For example, what if there were one right and flawless and utopian way to feed our kids?

Well, even then, being right does not give us the right to judge others who do not do things as we do. Jesus' commands to us apply at all times, as does the Bible's admonition to be kind and loving and gracious. All. The. Time.

So by all means, make decisions in the various areas of motherhood. Pray fervently. Converse with your husband, if you have one. Pick clean the brains of your experienced friends. Go with your gut. But trust God for your particular situation and don't expect that everyone else is going to do things your way. And when they don't? (Because they won't!) Be loving. Be gracious. Be supportive. Or at least be silent.

Of course be open to answering their questions, should they have any, about why you have come to the conclusion you have. But answer them with gentleness and respect. Let's do away with this notion that we are doing things the right and only way. Let's stop erecting fences that keep others out who don't behave just like us. Let's be bridge builders instead.

Now, on to our third myth ...

Myth #3: I Am "Just" a Mom

Oh no you are not! You are so, so, so much more!

It is a fact that a woman who cares for her children is doing something important in society. It is a lie that she is not doing something personally fulfilling. And it is a tall tale that it doesn't really matter to your children whether or not you are intentionally present in their life. Being a mom is so much more than just a default setting of a woman who couldn't get a "real" job.

If you have given up a career—or perhaps just put one on hold for a while or scaled back on your hours—in order to be more available to your family, you have done a wonderful thing. Full-time parenting is not for everyone, of course. Everyone's situation differs. God's hands are not tied, making him unable to work in the hearts and homes of those who have a mom who works outside the home part- or full-time. But if you are fortunate enough to have the financial means, and/or the support of your family, to be at home caring for your children, you have not sold out. You are not "less than." You are not a slough-off in society. You are performing a very valuable role! Remember, the hand that rocks the cradle rules the world.

A mother is crucial. These years are lightning fast and can only be lived once. While some days may feel as if they last for an eternity, the years certainly do fly by faster than the flutter of a hummingbird's wings. You cannot live them again. So make the most of them. Drink in every moment that you get to spend with your children, but don't lose yourself in the process. And don't buy the lie that you are not contributing to society and that what you are doing does not matter. It does.

It matters to your children. It matters to your entire family. And it matters to God. So many great saints of the faith and leaders in our world can trace their success back to the fact that they had an involved and praying mother in their life. Abraham Lincoln said, "All that I am, or hope to be, I owe to my angel Mother."

Okay. Although a mother is valuable and nearly irreplaceable, motherhood should not be the be-all and end-all of our lives. Which leads us to our next myth . . .

MYTH #4: MOTHERHOOD IS ALL-CONSUMING AND ALL-FULFILLING

[Buzzer sound] Wrong again. There will be times that you simply don't enjoy wearing the nametag of "Mom." You may even wonder

why you decided to have or adopt the munchkins in the first place! And being someone's mom should not be the sole focus of your entire existence—placing all your eggs in the "Best Mom Ever" basket. Only our relationship with God should consume and fulfill us. It is the only relationship that can't ever be plucked from us and which will last into eternity.

The sooner we accept that it really is a myth that we will feel fulfilled at all times being someone's mom, and that this role must take up all our time and energy—with none left over for other pursuits—the better it will be for us and for our children. We will learn to give ourselves a break. And some grace. We will begin to seek out snippets of time to keep alive our interests and passions and to invest in relationships with those outside of our home. And we will be approachable. Other moms will know we are a safe place to process their disappointments in motherhood, as together we point each other to our relationship with God for our identity and fulfillment.

MYTH #5: A GOOD MOTHER CAN DO IT ALL, ALL AT ONCE

All of the expectations placed on the shoulders of a mom today are enough to topple her over and send her into a deep funk. We simply cannot do it all. At least not all at once. And even if we do sequence things in our life, trying to eke out many experiences and opportunities, we were never made to be Supermom.

We were made to follow Christ.

Following Christ means we go to him for our motherhood marching orders. It means we recognize that he has gifted us in certain areas and yet, in other arenas, we are sorely lacking. As we learn to walk more closely in step with him, we discover what our passions and desires and areas of expertise are, what we were created to do. Then we can concentrate on these areas and stop letting the world call the shots, telling us all that we should be doing in order to be a "good mom."

We also need to let go of the notion that we are not allowed to farm out certain things. Or that we are not allowed to have our husbands pick up the slack. When we place these nostalgic and unrealistic expectations upon ourselves to be the ultimate homemaker, the wisest mother, the most conscientious community member, *and* the most loving wife all at once, we will send ourselves into a tizzy. No one can live up to those expectations! And it is okay to call in for backup sometimes.

Make sure you look to the Lord for how to handle all the responsibilities of raising your children. Don't look to your sister-in-law. Or the women in your Bible study. Or the mom in the playgroup. Or the one sipping her latte next to you on the soccer field. You do not have to be who they are or do what they do.

You are unique. God has given you children who are unique. Your situation is one-of-a-kind, and he is faithful to show you how to get done all that needs to be done to properly mother your children.

Trust God. Survey your family. Find a unique rhythm and routine that works for you and your family, and then do it with gusto! But don't try to do it all. You will only end up feeling discouraged and wanting to quit. You were never meant to take on a task so large. You are just one woman.

One woman with a very powerful God. The two of you are enough. No superhero needed.

Myth #6: Motherhood Is a Rat Race

Ask any mom how she is feeling and she will usually respond with "tired, busy, overwhelmed," etc. Yes, motherhood will test and try you in ways you never could have imagined. Your life will seem like a whirlwind at times. But the truth is that it doesn't have to stay that way.

We've been hoodwinked to believe that motherhood has to rule our lives. We don't have to believe the myth that this season of our life is out of control, crazy, and exhausting. While it is a busy and stressful season, there are steps we can take to live more on purpose. We can choose to live on mission, say no, and proactively face our schedules with what matters most. Motherhood doesn't have to be a rat race!

Myth #7: Motherhood Is the Luck of the Draw

You are not just "giving it your best shot!" Motherhood isn't about stumbling through the dark as you are raising a family. God has called you and equipped you to live with a mission to shape your children. God has given us his Word to inspire us and inform us so we don't have to guess at it.

The truth is that God has purposefully chosen you to be your child's mom. Raising your children has eternal value. Training, encouraging, shaping, teaching, and correcting your children to love God and love others requires a lot of work.

Don't be hoodwinked. Motherhood is not a shot in the dark. God has graciously called us to help pass on faith to the next generation. The good news is that we don't have to do this alone!

Myth #8: Everything Depends on Me

Yes, you are important. You are the first and most crucial teacher, mentor, and molder of your child's heart and soul. However, you are not their everything. You cannot possibly do and be and provide all that your child will need in life. Not when they are young. Not when they are teens.

In fact, remember, if you could meet all of your child's needs, they would have no need for God. Let's pinky-promise each other that we will no longer try to be everything to our offspring, but instead we will seek to make the most of every opportunity, to connect them to the people whom God has already chosen, to shape them into the people he wants them to be.

Get to know their passions. Discuss their interests vocationally or recreationally, even when they are very young. Make it a matter of prayer, this connecting of them to others who can teach them a skill, provide guidance, or offer encouragement. Be content to play the role God has for you in their life as their mother. You don't need to play each part in the entire supporting cast!

Got it? Good.

And now, let's talk about recipes. Cooking up a recipe for raising a stellar child. That is what our ninth myth is all about. A pinch of this, a dash of that. We have to measure carefully or we will screw up, right?

WRONG!

Let's tear down this one at its very base:

Myth #9: I Have to Do It All Right, or My Child Will Turn Out Wrong

Have you ever known someone who is a kind soul, always thinking of others? Or perhaps a man who is brave, fearless, a champion for the underdog and the downtrodden? Maybe another person who was at the top of their field academically, or intellectually, or even athletically? Know a conscientious nurse? A caring pastor? A loving teacher or thoughtful mail carrier?

I have known one person in each of these categories mentioned. Know what they all had in common?

They all had a bad upbringing.

Parents who were aloof. Or even absent. Neglectful. Even abusive. Some of the most wonderful and amazing people I know actually had a horrible childhood and parents who would not win any awards for the way they raised their children. (Or perhaps *didn't* raise their children. They let the schools and society do it. Or the kids sorta raised themselves!)

Now, of course this doesn't mean we should mess up on purpose. It just means that there isn't always a six-step recipe that ensures that our children turn out perfectly. And it also means that we don't have to do everything right for our children to turn out okay. We need to let go of the fear that if we make a parental misstep, our children are doomed to turn out wrong.

We have got to stop connecting the dots between what we do and how our children turn out. Or doing it in the reverse order and drawing an arrow from their behaviors straight back to our mothering.

If I am responsible for all of my child's actions, then that makes them a puppet. And God did not make puppets. He made people. At some point our children will make their own choices about how they live their lives. We hope that we have been a good influence on them and steered them in the right direction. But we cannot bank on any guarantees. And therefore, we should let go of this gripping fear that if we make even a slight wobble in our parenting, our child will suddenly become a serial killer.

(Okay, okay ... I know I exaggerate. But you know what I mean! Don't tell me you have not beat yourself up a time or two because you felt like you committed a parenting flop and wondered what irreparable harm it would impose on your dear offspring.)

So let's stop with trying to find that flawless recipe. It does not exist. Parenting is not a recipe. Parenting is a relationship. A relationship with Christ and with our children. As we grow in our vertical relationship with the Lord, we will also grow in our relationship with our children. Yes, we will make mistakes. Yes, we will regret what we say or do sometimes. However, if our children see us continually going back to Christ when we blow it or giving him credit when we do make a wise choice, they too may want to have a relationship with him, one that is alive and active and growing.

So let's tear up those recipe cards. Toss the maternal cookbooks. Log off the "how to raise perfect kids" websites. Run to Jesus. Both when you fail, and when you get it right.

Now finally ... oh, sisters, we *so need* to toss this final lie as far away from our mama hearts as our little arms can throw it. It is the myth that points its finger accusingly at us in our lowest times of parenting and tempts us to believe the following statement:

Myth #10: My Child's Bad Choice Means I'm a Bad Mom

All right. Maybe if your child is four years old and wandering around town in a sub-zero blizzard because (a) you forgot to put a coat on her that day and (b) you allowed her to stroll aimlessly about unsupervised, then yes, that may reflect poorly on you as a mom. But this is not what we are talking about when we mention this myth.

We are talking about when a child makes a choice. A slightly bad choice. Or a horrid one. You are not their choices. You must deal with the fallout of their choices, but you should not let their poor decisions define you.

Did your toddler strong-arm a kid in the play area at the local fast food eatery one day? Well, then they need to learn this behavior is unacceptable and will cost them a consequence. It does not, however, mean you need to shrink in shame, because this equation is *not* true: Roughhousing three-year-old + a pushing incident in the ball pit at Mickey D's = a bad mom.

Later, when they are older, they are going to make decisions that are not at all what you'd desire for them to make. While the magnitude of these choices may vary, *all* kids choose poorly sometimes. Do not strap your identity to the imperfect decisions of your kids. Their choices are their own. Help them learn from them, make amends for them, and not repeat them, but do not beat yourself up for them! And remember, when you want them the least is when they need you the most!

Ten myths. Ten mind frames we must shake.

Hoodwinked No More

Creeeeeak. Thunk. Creeeeeak. Thunk.

So went the old wooden door on the coffeehouse every time someone new came in or a patron left with their freshly custom-made beverage.

There at a round corner table, a few friends and I (Karen) gathered for a cup of something hot and delicious to sip while we visited on a fall afternoon and caught up with each other. We shared the ups and downs of our current lives as women, wives, and moms.

I'd known all these ladies for over two decades. We'd first forged our friendships as newlyweds, new moms, and for some, even as new followers of Jesus. We had bonded over pregnancy particulars, birthing tips—and a few horror stories—and the latest and greatest advice for raising toddlers or getting finicky kids to eat their steamed veggies. These girls were my team, my support system that I'd relied on in the early days of mothering when I was clueless, restless, and sometimes feeling hopeless as well.

Most of these dear friends were a bit ahead of me in the excursion of motherhood, having been married longer and been mothers longer than I had been. I was so grateful for our companionship over the years. They had been there for me through joys and concerns, often answering questions for me or giving me advice when I hit a mothering issue and did not know what to do.

As we sipped our lattes and nibbled on a few slices of biscotti we'd purchased to share, I glanced around at the faces of my friends. We'd all grown older, obviously, with laugh lines and age spots beginning to appear faintly on some.

When we first became a group of girlfriends, we all still had our natural hair color. Now I was pretty sure all of us touched up our gray roots regularly, although only our hairdressers would know for sure. Our hands had cared for children—and for aging parents. Our feet and hearts had walked through difficulties in marriage, and our eyes had seen some of our children begin to walk away from the Lord.

My mind migrated back to our early days, the times when we all used to gather at the playground or Sunday school outings and such. Our kids were so young. And really, so were we. Back then, we were optimistic about how our offspring would turn out one day. We had high hopes and a deep faith in God. We wanted to raise sons and daughters who would love and serve both him and others, who would rise above the ordinary and resist the urge to be typical and "normal," who would stand out as servants of Christ.

And for some of our kids, that is exactly what happened. But not for all of them. Perhaps none of us would ever have dreamed all that would eventually come of our children — things that would happen to them both by choice and by chance. And certainly there were some circumstances we would never wish on anyone.

As we chatted and brought each other up to speed, we also shared news of other friends who had not joined us that day. Some had moved away. Most were still in the area. Nearly all of them too had lives that had taken sudden twists and turns they never saw coming.

When I took a quick inventory of my fellow moms, both those who were sitting with me and others who were in my thoughts, I realized that at least one of us had experienced the following either in our immediate or extended families, many in the lives of our now teenaged or adult children:

- Serious sickness requiring hospitalization or long-term medication or care
- Car accidents, one caused by a teenage son resulting in a lawsuit that could have potentially cost my friend her home
- Mental illness in an adult child that seemed to come out of nowhere, resulting in anger, bitterness, and even a short period of homelessness for that child
- Teen rebellion, including experimenting with tobacco, alcohol, and illegal drugs
- A tragic auto accident that left a child in a wheelchair for life
- Sons or daughters being caught with inappropriate images on their cell phones
- Children caught lying or stealing
- A child diagnosed with a serious learning disability that required expensive therapy just to get him through high school

❀ A husband who did not fare well in mid-life and looked elsewhere to satisfy his sexual desires

❀ A child who revealed to an unsuspecting family that he was unashamedly living a sexually immoral lifestyle

❀ Job loss and/or long-term layoffs for them or their husbands

❀ Moms who swore they'd homeschool only but then put their kids in public school

❀ Moms who swore they'd never homeschool but who pulled their kids from public school to teach them at home

❀ A daughter with a serious and life-threatening eating disorder

❀ Married children whose newfound political views or opinions on social issues differed greatly from their parents, causing tension and even, in one case, a fractured relationship

❀ Aging parents who required extra care or a place to live in old age, and so moved in with a child and needed round-the-clock attention

❀ An unwanted and unexpected divorce after an affair was discovered

❀ An offspring facing prison time

❀ The death of a teen in a freak accident at work

❀ Foreclosure on a home

Now, if that list of life occurrences had been presented to me or to any of my friends when we embarked on the journey of motherhood, we would have run away as quickly as our little legs could have taken us. No way would we have seen any good in these situations! Just thinking I might experience even one of them would have rattled my soul. After all, I was going to do the right things. The righteous things. And then my kids would all turn out right, and righteous too. It was a simple formula. A recipe for spiritual success. If we just fed, disciplined, schooled, and molded our kids in a certain way, triumph was sure to be ours!

But sitting here as we all shared our stories and caught each other up on the details of our lives, including what was happening in our marriages and with our children—and for some, even grandchildren—well, the scenarios didn't play out at all like we had hoped they would.

You'd think we'd be sad. Dejected. Feeling hopeless or at least discouraged. But that was not the case.

One by one, as I glanced around at the faces of my friends, I saw women—strong women. Wives and mothers who had trudged through some great difficulties in life but were better for it. These were women to whom I would go when I had an issue as minor as how to remove a nasty grass stain from my child's light-colored pants, but also with whom I would trust my deepest spiritual questions. They were moms I could be assured would give me a good and godly answer, because they had traveled tight with Jesus.

Our individual and collective journeys were not some stroll in the park through life. We were not happily skipping along, chaperoned by a magician-like God who granted our every wish. Not by a long shot.

This journey was more like a grueling hike up and down treacherous mountains. A march in the middle of the darkest night with an unknown destination. A voyage through enemy territory that seemed scary and unsure. But these women had walked faithfully with God.

Because I had seen them face much adversity and have life's rug ripped out from under them more than a time or two, I could trust them. I knew I was not going to get any Sunday-school answers from them. No pie-in-the-sky platitudes or rose-colored-glasses outlook on life. I could trust them to shoot straight with me.

And shoot straight they did.

One by one, as we continued to share, I could see a pattern emerging as they talked about life. About God. About their relationship with him.

Although the journey of motherhood and marriage had not been easy, it had been so worth it. I doubt a single one of them would've traded the spiritual depth they feel now for an easy-breezy life and perfect children and husbands. No. It is in the heat of conflict and the depths of despair where we forge a solid relationship with Christ.

Once upon a time, we foolishly thought we had it all figured out. Now we know only God knows everything. Only he can be everything—to us as moms and also to our kids. And it is in our total reliance on him for our lifestyles and answers that we grow a deep faith, one that finds us throwing ourselves on Jesus, saturating ourselves with God's Word, and raising our kids on our knees as deep in prayer as we are in laundry and homework and life.

So run to him, mom. Run away from the myths. Jump with abandon into the arms of the Truth himself. The Way. The Truth. And the Life. Like a loving father who has gained his toddler's complete trust. Run. Jump. Land and be held.

The ride is sometimes scary. The twists and turns play games with our insides until we aren't quite sure how much more we can stomach. But he is faithful. Always faithful. He will never leave you to walk alone but will carry you each step of the way, if only you will let him.

We believe in you, mom. Be hoodwinked no more. Let the truth of these words sink into your soul.

And then … love lavishly and mother well.

Will you allow us the honor of praying for you?

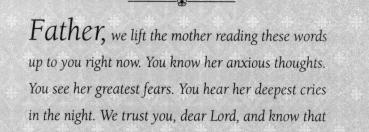

Father, we lift the mother reading these words up to you right now. You know her anxious thoughts. You see her greatest fears. You hear her deepest cries in the night. We trust you, dear Lord, and know that

you always know what is best for us and for our kids. You do not make mistakes. There is nothing that takes you by surprise. Each child. Each situation. Each joy and each sorrow are all allowed in our lives on purpose. May they not make us fretful. May they not make us bitter. May they not cause us to give up but to walk ever closer with you. We want to believe the truth. And live the truth. Because you, O Lord, are the Truth that frees us. The Way that steers us. And the very Life—exceedingly abundant and gloriously everlasting. Into your care we place our fears and commit our children's future. We love you, our Father. Please perfectly parent us as we mother, freed from all the myths and tethered to the Truth. Amen.

Bonus Material

We hope this section will be an encouragement to you and equip you in your mothering. We have included some practical material, including a yearly personal inventory, a mother's prayer for her child, a mother's week of prayer prompts, ten memory verses for the too-busy mom, and minute-long mom pep talks excerpted from the book. Feel free to copy any of the material and cut it out to carry with you or post in a prominent place to help you to commit it to memory. We believe these resources will help, because we believe in you!

Yearly Personal Inventory for Moms

We wholeheartedly recommend that at least once a year you carve out some time to be alone and work your way through this inventory of questions. Perhaps you can trade babysitting with a friend so that each of you will have a few hours to be alone in your thoughts—and with God—to craft your answers. Take along your Bible and read slowly through the following Scripture passage before answering the questions.

> Search me, God, and know my heart;
>> test me and know my anxious thoughts.
> See if there is any offensive way in me,
>> and lead me in the way everlasting.
>
> (Psalm 139:23–24)

1. How would you describe your life right now? What would you like to change?

   _____

   _____

   _____

   _____

2. How are you emotionally? What emotions or feelings are most often present in your life right now?

   _____

   _____

   _____

   _____

3. How are you taking care of your health? What do you need to change in the areas of sleep, exercise, nutrition, and rest and relaxation?

_____

_____

_____

_____

_____

4. How are you doing spiritually? How is your devotional life? What goals do you have for your devotional life over the next year?

_____

_____

_____

_____

5. What is your greatest need in your marriage right now? What goals can you and your husband establish for your marriage?

_____

_____

_____

_____

6. What is your greatest need as a mom right now? Where are you struggling? How can you better embrace your calling?

_____

_____

_____

_____

7. How are your children doing? What character qualities in your kids do you want to cultivate most this year?

_____

_____

_____

_____

_____

8. What commitments or activities do you need to let go of this year? What opportunities do you need to take hold of this year?

_____

_____

_____

_____

_____

9. What personal character quality do you need to cultivate most over the next year?

_____

_____

_____

_____

_____

10. How would you best summarize what God is calling you to focus on most and do this year?

_____

_____

_____

_____

_____

A Mother's Prayer
for Her Child

The following is one of our favorite passages of Scripture. We want you to take a moment and pray this passage of God's Word with your children in mind. You'll notice there are several blanks—this is where you insert your child's name. May God use this to encourage your heart as you shape your children. As you parent, don't forget that God is the Master Shaper and Artist.

Psalm 139:13–18, author's paraphrase

For you created _____'s inmost being; you knit _____ together in my womb.

I praise you because _____ is fearfully and wonderfully made; your works are wonderful, I know that full well.

_____'s frame was not hidden from you when he/she was made in the secret place, when _____ was woven together in the depths of the earth.

Your eyes saw _____'s unformed body; all the days ordained for him/her were written in your book before one of them came to be.

How precious to me are your thoughts, God! How vast is the sum of them!

Were I to count them, they would outnumber the grains of sand—when I awake, I am still with you.

A Mother's Week of Prayer Prompts

We encourage you to use this little weekly chart to help you focus on seven areas of your life as a mom, intentionally making them a matter of prayer. Perhaps you would like to purchase a journal to record your prayers—and God's responses—on its pages. Or set up a prayer notebook with a three-ring binder and plastic page protectors as used in scrapbooking. You can photocopy the following prayer prompts to put in page protectors at the beginning of the notebook. (If you are the crafty sort, use decorative paper or place a picture of your family in this section.)

After that, make seven pages, each one listing a day of the week. You could make these pages simple, handwritten ones or kick it up a notch and make them with decorative scrapbooking paper and photos. Customize them any way you'd like. Then, place plenty of blank paper in each section just behind each day-of-the-week page. Each day, as you spend a few moments in quiet reflection, jot down one or more of the prayer prompts to help you pen your prayers to God on the blank pages.

❧ MONDAY ❧

My Mama-Heart Cries:
Praying for My Children

Father, _____ is really on my heart today because _____. Will you please empower him/her to _____?

Jesus, _____ needs to know you are near today and that you love him/her. Will you orchestrate a situation today that will show him/her how much you care for them?

Dear God, _____ is really struggling with _____. Please show me clearly how I can come alongside her/him in this struggle to help and not to hinder.

Father, which of my kids needs a special touch this week from me as their mom? Show me what I am to do to let him/her know how very deeply I love and care for them.

Jesus, this week my child _____ will face _____. Show me how I am to pray for this situation.

These Tangled-Up Emotions: Praying for a Sound Mind

Father, right now my heart feels full of the emotion of
_____. Will you help me to sort out this
emotion today? Why am I feeling this way? What do you say
about this emotion? Please help me to search your Word and
record helpful thoughts here.

❀

Lord, a situation happened that has hurt my heart. It is this:

_____

_____

_____

_____

_____

❀

I sense you telling me the following about the situation that
has wounded my heart:

_____

_____

_____

_____

_____

❀

Help me to choose a passage of Scripture below to meditate on today as I deal with my feelings about this issue:

> How long, LORD? Will you forget me forever? How long will you hide your face from me? How long must I wrestle with my thoughts and day after day have sorrow in my heart? How long will my enemy triumph over me? Look on me and answer, LORD my God.
>
> (PSALM 13:1–3)

> Turn to me and be gracious to me, for I am lonely and afflicted. Relieve the troubles of my heart and free me from my anguish. Look on my affliction and my distress and take away all my sins.
>
> (PSALM 25:16–18)

> Therefore, since we have a great high priest who has ascended into heaven, Jesus the Son of God, let us hold firmly to the faith we profess. For we do not have a high priest who is unable to empathize with our weaknesses, but we have one who has been tempted in every way, just as we are—yet he did not sin. Let us then approach God's throne of grace with confidence, so that we may receive mercy and find grace to help us in our time of need.
>
> (HEBREWS 4:14–16)

Working on My Walk:
Praying for My Spiritual Growth

Father, I long to grow daily to be more like you. Please show me an area of my life that I need to work on for this growth to take place: _____
_____

❈

One prayer I have about my time spent in your Word is:
_____
_____

❈

One prayer I have about talking to others about my faith this week is: _____
_____

❈

A question or struggle I am having with my prayer life currently is:_____
_____

❈

I want to make more time to memorize Scripture. A verse I would like to commit to memory is:_____
_____

⚛️ THURSDAY ⚛️

Taking My Tasks Before Him: Praying for My Home

Father, one of the tasks of motherhood that I am wrestling with right now is _____ because of: _____

_____

———— ✿ ————

Dear Lord, whenever it comes time to _____ around the house, I feel so frustrated! Help me to sort out my thoughts on this issue now: _____

_____

———— ✿ ————

Jesus, an area of home life that I know I am neglecting is _____. Please help me to gain a renewed perspective in this area. I pour out my feelings to you about this here: _____

_____

———— ✿ ————

Father, will you enable me to find joy in serving my family and tackling the often thankless tasks of motherhood? Help me to list here reasons why serving you by serving my family matters: _____

_____

∼◈ FRIDAY ◈∼

Forging Faithful Friendships:
Praying for My Soul Sisters

Father, some qualities I think are crucial in a good friend are:

_____

_____

———— ❈ ————

Now, of the above qualities I've listed, the one I personally
need to work on most is _____.
The person with whom I need to concentrate on this with is

_____.

———— ❈ ————

Dear God, a friend who is on my heart today is

_____ because: _____
———— ❈ ————

One action I can take to reach out to this friend in the next
week or so is:_____

Father God, your Word says that a friend loves at all times
(Proverbs 17:17). Right now I am having a hard time loving
_____ because of this situation:

_____

———— ❈ ————

Reveal to me what I need to do in order to love this person
well. Do I need to reach out and have a conversation with
her? Write a note of apology? Simply spend some time listening to her? What I sense you are calling me to do in this
friendship is: _____

❧ SATURDAY ❧

Simplifying Life:
Praying through My Schedule

Jesus, one aspect of my current schedule that is causing me great grief is: _____

———❀———

What might I do differently in order to deal with this current hassle? Help me to jot down some possible solutions now:

_____

———❀———

Father, here are the ongoing commitments I currently have in my life:_____

———❀———

And these are the one-time commitments I have coming up on my plate this week or very soon: _____

———❀———

Lord, help me to pray back over these two lists carefully and with a heart of honesty, asking you if I need to let go of any of these commitments. I will record my thoughts about this here after praying: _____

———❀———

On the flip side, is there something you are nudging me to take on in my schedule? If so, what is it? _____

———❀———

How will I need to adjust my schedule and commitments in order to say yes to what you call me to do and no to all other requests?

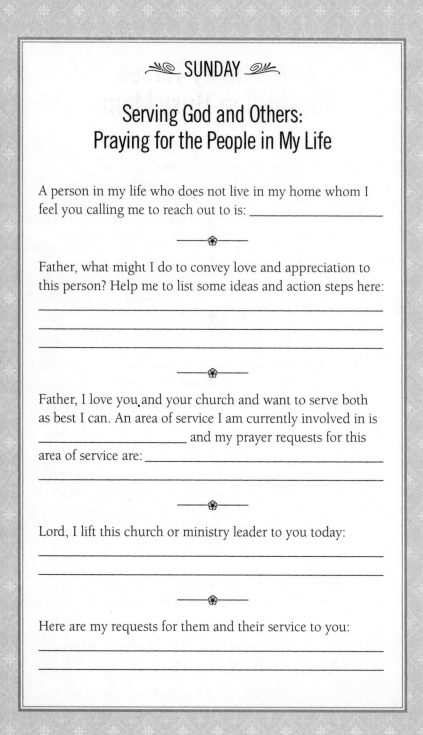

✎ SUNDAY ✎

Serving God and Others:
Praying for the People in My Life

A person in my life who does not live in my home whom I
feel you calling me to reach out to is: _____

———— ✿ ————

Father, what might I do to convey love and appreciation to
this person? Help me to list some ideas and action steps here:

_____

_____

_____

———— ✿ ————

Father, I love you and your church and want to serve both
as best I can. An area of service I am currently involved in is
_____ and my prayer requests for this
area of service are: _____

_____

———— ✿ ————

Lord, I lift this church or ministry leader to you today:

_____

_____

———— ✿ ————

Here are my requests for them and their service to you:

_____

_____

Ten Memory Verses
for the Too-Busy Mom

Here are a few verses to commit to memory that will help you to pause and pray when you feel tempted to take on too much—or that will help you to slow down and rest in the Lord. They are sized the same as a business card so you can photocopy them on card stock and keep them in a card holder to carry with you.

But if from there you seek the LORD your God, you will find him if you seek him with all your heart and with all your soul.

(DEUTERONOMY 4:29)

Those who know your name trust in you, for you, LORD, have never forsaken those who seek you.

(PSALM 9:10)

But I trust in you, Lord; I say, "You are my God." My times are in your hands.

(Psalm 31:14–15)

Look to the Lord and his strength; seek his face always.

(1 Chronicles 16:11)

"Ask and it will be given to you; seek and you will find; knock and the door will be opened to you. For everyone who asks receives; the one who seeks finds; and to the one who knocks, the door will be opened."

(Matthew 7:7–8)

Very early in the morning, while it was still dark, Jesus got up, left the house and went off to a solitary place, where he prayed.

(MARK 1:35)

Answer me when I call to you, my righteous God. Give me relief from my distress; have mercy on me and hear my prayer.

(PSALM 4:1)

"Come to me, all you who are weary and burdened, and I will give you rest."

(MATTHEW 11:28)

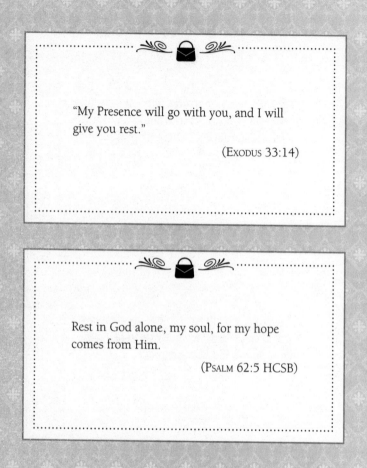

"My Presence will go with you, and I will give you rest."

(EXODUS 33:14)

Rest in God alone, my soul, for my hope comes from Him.

(PSALM 62:5 HCSB)

Minute-Long Mom Pep Talks from Hoodwinked

Here are some sections of the book pulled out for you to photocopy and place where you can see them often. We pray these little pep talks will help you to find and maintain your perspective as you mother your children.

We moms are never going to get everything perfect. Not our homes. Not our method of discipline. Not our food. Not our schedule. When we keep these mythical mosaics of perfection as our goal, we only set ourselves up for sure failure. We need to stop pursuing the appearance of perfection. (Yes, the *appearance* of perfection. There is no such thing as actual perfection.) We must start instead to pursue the person Jesus Christ.

------❁------

God has set apart the home as his. Home is a place where his presence is to be felt and his purposes are to be pursued. He places parents in those homes as watchmen, pastors, priests, shepherds, teachers, and warriors who have been called and commissioned to pass on their faith to their children for the sake of the world.

------❁------

Of course, take pleasure being a mom. It will bring you delight often. However, true joy comes from serving Jesus. If you hang your hat of happiness on being a mom, you will experience despair during the down times or when your child isn't making good and godly choices. Get your true joy from being a follower of Jesus, not from being the mom of so-and-so.

------❁------

The importance of what we do for God is not contingent upon how many *people* see what we do. God measures our faithfulness to him (and our families) the same, whether others see it or not. Is the "divine nod" of the God who sees enough for you?

Rules may change behavior, but they cannot change the heart. Our children need our love and not just our law.

If we want our children to be disciples of Jesus, then we must first be parents who are disciples of Jesus. You will pass on what you possess.

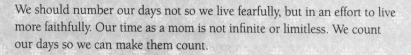

We should number our days not so we live fearfully, but in an effort to live more faithfully. Our time as a mom is not infinite or limitless. We count our days so we can make them count.

Do not tether your identity to the choices of your child, whether stellar or stupid. We are not our child's choices. Their choices and their behavior are their own.

Parenting is not a recipe. Parenting is a relationship. A relationship with Christ and with our children. As we grow in our vertical relationship with the Lord, we will also grow in our relationship with our children. Yes, we will make mistakes. Yes, we will regret what we say or do sometimes. However, if our children see us continually going back to Christ when we blow it or giving him credit when we do make a wise choice, they too may want to have a relationship with him, one that is alive and active and growing. So let's tear up those recipe cards. Toss the maternal cookbooks. Log off the "how to raise perfect kids" websites. Run to Jesus. Both when you fail, and when you get it right.

Acknowledgments

From Karen:

To my husband, Todd, and kids, Kenna, Mitch, and Spence: I'm so grateful that I am both the Mrs. and the mom of this crazy bunch! I love you and I like you too.

To my own mom, Margaret Patterson, who raised my brother and me on her knees while also providing for us materially. You made it look so easy, yet always gave God the credit. Thank you for teaching me to take life one day at a time.

To my Proverbs 31 Ministries sisters, especially our president Lysa TerKeurst: thank you for allowing me to strike the balance between being a worker and a wife and a mother. You are such great examples of how to walk that delicate line in a way that glorifies God, and him alone.

To Ruth: I love doing ministry with you and encouraging moms together. Who would have thought a simple meeting at a coffee shop would turn into this project! Thanks for working hard and laughing often. It certainly kept us going. (Well, that and coffee and Nutella.)

To so many of my fellow mom-friends who over the years modeled for me how to mother well: Kelly Hovermale, Marcia Stump, Suzy Williams, Debi Davis, Andie Cocco, Tammy Underwood, Trisha Hufnagel, Jill Savage, Julie Barnhill, and especially my Good Morning Girls, Mary Steinke, Kim Cordes, Sharon Glasgow, and Lindsey Feldpausch.

From Ruth:

I am in awe and so very thankful that God chose to use an ordinary girl like me to spread his message of hope, light, and love to this world. *Blessed* doesn't even begin to describe how I feel to be able to share this message of truth with moms.

Thank you to my amazing husband, who has cheered me on and supported me for the last seventeen years of marriage. God couldn't have made anyone more perfect for me than you. I love you.

Tyler, Bella, Noah, and Sophia, I am so thankful to be your mom. You make motherhood easy. You have blessed my life and I am so very proud of each of you. I love you.

Thank you to my parents, who believed I could change the world from the moment I was born. Your support, love, and unending encouragement have inspired me to work hard and dream huge. I love you.

Thank you to the mom who changed my whole view on motherhood ten years ago: Sally Clarkson. Your example and voice of truth has inspired me countless times. I love you dearly and am thankful to call you my mentor and friend.

Thank you to my dear mentor and friend, Sandra Maddox. I am beyond blessed to have you in my life. God gave me the special mentor, "second mom," and friend that I needed in you.

Thank you, Karen Ehman, for partnering with and taking a chance on me. I couldn't have asked for a better coauthor or a crazier friend! I love all of our silly Voxes and late-night chats.

Thank you to my online-turned-real-life friends who have prayed for me, laughed with me, cried with me, and cheered for me. You know who you are. I can't imagine doing life without each of you. You have become my closest confidants and my dearest allies.

Thank you to The Better Mom and For the Family team of contributors. I am blessed every day to do ministry with you and to call you my friends.

Thank you to the readers of The Better Mom and For the Family. I am blessed to be on this journey with each one of you and am so very thankful for your support. I pray every day that God would work tremendously in your lives and you would be inspired to raise generations that will impact the world for Christ.

From Karen and Ruth:

Thank you to Esther Fedorkevich, our agent, for your creativity, persistence, and confidence in this project. Your drive and encouragement is a breath of fresh air.

Thank you, Sandy Vander Zicht, and the rest of the team at Zondervan, including Robin Phillips, Londa Alderink, and editor extraordinaire Lori Vanden Bosch. We are so thankful for your guidance and encouragement. We couldn't have asked for a better team. Thank you for your tireless commitment to spreading this message of hope to moms.

Notes

1. Jessica Valenti, "Not Wanting Kids Is Perfectly Normal," *The Atlantic*, September 19, 2012. http://www.theatlantic.com/health/archive/2012/09/not-wanting-kids-is-entirely-normal/262367/.

2. Richard Foster, *The Celebration of Discipline*, 3rd ed. (San Francisco: HarperSanFrancisco, 2002), 128.

3. Lysa TerKeurst, *The Best Yes* (Nashville: Thomas Nelson, 2014), 10.

4. Frederick Buechner, *The Hungering Dark* (San Francisco: HarperOne, 1985), 74.

5. Warren Wiersbe, *The Wiersbe Bible Commentary: Old Testament* (Colorado Springs: David C. Cook, 2007), 67.

6. Scott Dannemiller, "The One Question Every Parent Should Quit Asking," *The Huffington Post*, November 20, 2014, *http://www.huffingtonpost.com/scott-dannemiller/the-one-question-every-parent-should-quit-asking_b_6182248.html*.

7. Dr. Leonard Sax, *Boys Adrift* (New York: Basic Books, 2009), 42–47.

8. George Barna, *Revolutionary Parenting* (Carol Stream, Ill.: Tyndale, 2010), 15.

About the Authors

Karen Ehman is a Proverbs 31 Ministries speaker, a *New York Times* bestselling author, and a writer for *Encouragement for Today*, an online devotional that reaches over one million women daily. She has written eight books including *Keep It Shut: What to Say, How to Say It & When to Say Nothing at All*. Married to her college sweetheart, Todd, and the mother of three, she enjoys antique hunting, cheering for the Detroit Tigers baseball team, and feeding the many teens who gather around her kitchen island for a taste of Mama Karen's cooking. Connect with her at www.karenehman.com.

Ruth Schwenk is the creator of The Better Mom website (www.thebettermom.com), and, along with her husband, the creator of For the Family (www.forthefamily.org), a site designed to equip and encourage parents. She is a pastor's wife, mom of four energetic kids, a lover of good coffee, and a dreamer of big dreams. She loves leading, speaking, blogging, and encouraging her audience to better themselves as they grow to be more like Christ. A graduate of Moody Bible Institute, Ruth has been serving with her husband full-time in local church ministry for over fifteen years.

Proverbs 31
MINISTRIES

ABOUT PROVERBS 31 MINISTRIES

Karen Ehman is an author, speaker, and online devotion writer for Proverbs 31 Ministries, located in Charlotte, North Carolina.

If you were inspired by *Hoodwinked* and desire to deepen your own personal relationship with Jesus Christ, we encourage you to connect with Proverbs 31 Ministries.

We exist to be a trusted friend who will take you by the hand and walk by your side, leading you one step closer to the heart of God through:

- Free online daily devotions
- Online Bible studies
- Daily radio programs
- Books and resources

For more information about Proverbs 31 Ministries, visit: www.Proverbs31.org.

To inquire about having Karen speak at your event, visit www.Proverbs31.org and click on "speakers."

the Better Mom
growing better together

Now that you have learned how to reject the lies and start walking in the truth in this journey of motherhood, wouldn't it be great to connect with other moms?

TheBetterMom.com is the place for you!

At The Better Mom our mission is to build God-honoring homes by inspiring moms to be better moms through sharing life and learning together.

We are moms who desire to be "better" even though we are busy. We believe God has placed a high calling on our lives as we:

- Raise children to impact the world
- Take care of our homes
- Love our husbands
- Ultimately honor God with our lives

We would love to have you join our community
and share in our journey!

Join us today at
www.TheBetterMom.com

Hoodwinked
DVD Study

Ten Myths Moms Believe & Why We All Need to Knock It Off

Karen Ehman and Ruth Schwenk

According to Karen Ehman, popular author and speaker with Proverbs 31 Ministries, and Ruth Schwenk, of TheBetterMom.com, it's time to stop the "Mommy Wars."

Today's wives and mothers have been hoodwinked, convinced that serving their family is a subservient and antiquated role. Because of culture, family, friends, or lack of biblical teaching, many moms miss how valuable and powerful their calling really is. Some have bought into the pressure to be Supermom. Others have believed the myth that they can "do it all" and do it perfectly.

This six-session video-based study (study guide sold separately or in a pack) will encourage and inspire women to embrace their roles as mothers wholeheartedly yet realistically, whether they work outside the home, have a home business, or are stay-at-home moms. Mothers will find a fresh new vision for an age-old calling as they tackle the challenges and embrace the blessings of motherhood.

Available in stores and online!

Keep It Shut

What to Say, How to Say It, and When to Say Nothing at All

Karen Ehman

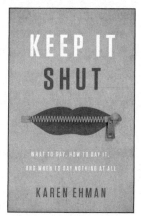

From Bible times to modern times, women have struggled with their words. What to say and how to say it. What not to say. When it is best to remain silent. And what to do when you've said something you wish you could now take back. In this book a woman whose mouth has gotten her into loads of trouble shares the hows (and how-not-tos) of dealing with the tongue.

Beyond just a "how not to gossip" book, this book explores what the Bible says about the many ways we are to use our words and the times when we are to remain silent. Karen will cover using our speech to interact with friends, coworkers, family, and strangers as well as in the many places we use our words in private, in public, online, and in prayer. Even the words we say silently to ourselves. She will address unsolicited opinion-slinging, speaking the truth in love, not saying words just to people-please, and dealing with our verbal anger.

Christian women struggle with their mouths. Even though we know that Scripture has much to say about how we are—and are not—to use our words, this is still an immense issue, causing heartache and strain not only in family relationships, but also in friendships, work, and church settings.

Six-session DVD study also available.

Available in stores and online!

Let. It. Go.

How to Stop Running the Show and Start Walking in Faith

Karen Ehman

Many women are wired to control. You're the ones who make sure the house is clean, the meals are prepared, the beds are made, the children are dressed, and everyone gets to work, school, and other activities on time.

But trying to control everything can be exhausting, and it can also cause friction with your friends and family.

This humorous, yet thought-provoking book guides you as you discover for yourself the freedom and reward of living a life "out of control," in which you allow God to be seated in the rightful place in your life. Armed with relevant biblical and current examples (both to emulate and to avoid), doable ideas, new thought patterns, and practical tools to implement, *Let. It. Go.* will gently lead you out of the land of over-control and into a place of quiet trust.

Six-session DVD study also available.

Available in stores and online!